Colorado
Bed
&
Breakfast
Cookbook

Acknowledgements

Creating a book is a work involving many people. We owe a great deal of gratitude to the following friends, family members and business colleagues for their support, inspiration, enthusiasm, time and talents:

Dave Rich, Melissa Craven, Nikki Van Thiel, Jory Payne, Doris Anderson, Erin Faino, Ole Sykes, our official taste-testers and a special thank you to the owners, innkeepers and chefs of the 88 Colorado bed and breakfasts who generously and enthusiastically shared their favorite recipes and beautiful artwork.

We want to express our love and heartfelt thanks to our parents, Margaret and Harold McCollum and Nan and Lawrence Kaitfors; our husbands, Rod Faino and Don Hazledine; and children, Kyle, Erin, Ryan and daughter-in-law Laura Faino, for their continued interest, ideas, feedback and support.

Table of Contents

Introduction

Many exciting events have occurred since we first published the *Colorado Bed & Breakfast Cookbook* back in 1996. Because of our never-waning fascination with B&Bs, we have continued to visit charming bed and breakfasts and country inns across the country and have tested hundreds of new recipes. The results are two beautiful additions to our cookbook and travel guide series: *The Washington State Bed & Breakfast Cookbook* and the *California Wine Country Bed & Breakfast Cookbook and Travel Guide*.

However, change has also occurred here in Colorado. Each year numerous innkeepers retire, yet at the same time many newcomers to the industry are enthusiastically embracing new careers as professional innkeepers, and sometimes even take on the additional challenge of building their own "dream inn."

We decided the time was right to update and revise our first edition of the *Colorado Bed & Breakfast Cookbook*. We added 36 wonderful new inns and 72 of their tempting recipes, and enhanced the B&B informational categories, which now include e-mail addresses, websites, handicapped accessibility and willingness to accommodate guests' special dietary needs. Proudly, we present our fourth book, the *Colorado Bed & Breakfast Cookbook, Second Edition*.

We eagerly look forward to starting the next book in our B&B series. Each state provides an exciting new adventure for us, as we discover more B&B treasures and learn about the popular foods of each region. We have come to the conclusion, however, that some things never change – wherever we go, two things remain constant. Innkeepers are very interesting people, and they delight in serving beautiful and bountiful breakfasts!

We love sharing what we learn. We hope you find this second edition as useful as the first when planning your travels to Colorado's finest B&B's and in recreating memorable dining moments using this treasure trove of recipes.

Happy Cooking!

Carol Faino & Doreen Hazledine

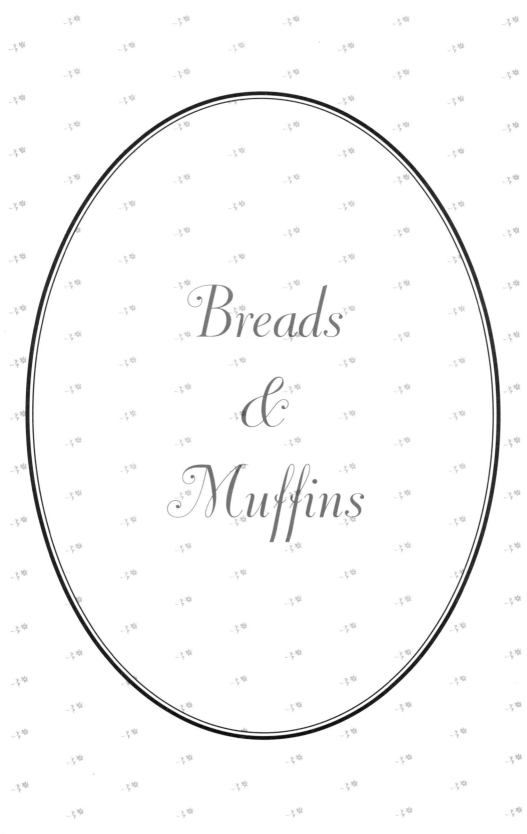

Breads
&
Muffins

Tudor Rose

The Tudor Rose is a stately, country manor located high on a piñon treed hill. The land surrounding this unique Tudor estate covers 37 sprawling acres that were once part of an 1890's homestead.

Remnants of the old homestead buildings and a hand-dug, stone-lined well still stand in the lower pasture, defiant of the passage of time.

INNKEEPERS:	Jon & Terre' Terrell
ADDRESS:	6720 Paradise Road; PO Box 89
	Salida, CO 81201
TELEPHONE:	(719) 539-2002; (800) 379-0889
E-MAIL:	info@thetudorrose.com
WEBSITE:	www.thetudorrose.com
ROOMS:	4 Rooms; 2 Suites; Private & shared baths
CHILDREN:	Children age 6 and older are welcome
ANIMALS:	Welcome; Fenced outdoor accommodations;
	Overnight stabling
HANDICAPPED:	Not handicapped accessible
DIETARY NEEDS:	Will accommodate guests' special dietary needs

Chocolate Bread with Raspberry Sauce

Makes 1 Loaf

2½ cups all-purpose flour
1½ teaspoons baking soda
½ cup unsweetened cocoa powder
1 cup sugar
½ teaspoon salt
1 egg, beaten
⅓ cup butter, melted
1¼ cups sour milk (see note below)
¾ cup walnuts, chopped
Smucker's natural red raspberry syrup
Fresh red raspberries

Preheat oven to 350°F. Grease and flour a 9x5-inch loaf pan. In a large bowl, sift together the first 5 ingredients. In a smaller bowl, combine the egg, melted butter and sour milk. Add the wet ingredients to the dry ingredients and stir just until blended. Fold in the nuts. Pour batter into the prepared loaf pan. Bake for 50-60 minutes, or until a toothpick inserted in the center of the bread comes out clean.

Presentation: Place a piece of warm chocolate bread on a small plate. Drizzle the syrup over the bread and around the plate. Garnish with raspberries.

Note: To make sour milk, put 1 tablespoon lemon juice or vinegar in a measuring cup, add enough milk (at room temperature) to make 1¼ cups. Allow mixture to sit for 5 minutes.

> **Carol's Corner**
> *This is perfect for a special breakfast. For a memorable dessert, top the bread with a big scoop of vanilla ice cream before adding the syrup and raspberries.*

Ambiance Inn

The Ambiance Inn is internationally recognized as one of the finest bed and breakfasts in the Rocky Mountain region. Set in pastoral Carbondale, half a block off Main Street, the inn is a contemporary chalet with spacious, comfortable rooms.

Year-round activities, just minutes from the inn, include Gold Medal fishing, whitewater rafting, golf, horseback riding and cross-country and alpine skiing.

INNKEEPERS:	Bob & Norma Morris
ADDRESS:	66 North Second Street
	Carbondale, CO 81623
TELEPHONE:	(970) 963-3597; (800) 350-1515
E-MAIL:	ambiancein@aol.com
WEBSITE:	www.ambianceinn.com
ROOMS:	4 Rooms; All with private baths
CHILDREN:	Children age 7 and older are welcome
ANIMALS:	Not allowed
HANDICAPPED:	Not handicapped accessible
DIETARY NEEDS:	Will accommodate guests' special dietary needs

Poppy Seed Bread

Makes 2 Loaves

2	cups sugar
1½	cups vegetable oil
3	eggs
1½	teaspoons vanilla extract
1½	teaspoons almond extract
3	cups flour
½	teaspoon salt
1½	teaspoons baking powder
2	tablespoons poppy seeds
1½	cups milk

Orange glaze (recipe below)

Preheat oven to 350°F. Grease and flour two 9x5-inch loaf pans. In a large bowl, cream together the sugar, oil, eggs and vanilla and almond extracts. Combine the flour, salt, baking powder and poppy seeds in a separate bowl.

Add the dry ingredients to the wet ingredients alternately with the milk, ending with the dry ingredients. Stir just until ingredients are combined (do not overmix). Divide batter equally between the two loaf pans.

Bake for 1 hour, or until a toothpick inserted in the center comes out clean. While the bread is still warm and in the pan, drizzle the orange glaze over the top of the loaves. Place on a wire rack until almost cool. Run a knife around the edges of the pans and remove the loaves. Finish cooling on a wire rack.

Orange glaze:

¼	cup orange juice
¾	cup sugar
½	teaspoon almond extract

Combine the orange juice, sugar and almond extract in a medium bowl.

Old Town Guest House

Perfect for the business traveler, the Old Town Guest House Bed and Breakfast is specifically designed as a corporate retreat. A private conference facility is available for meetings and special events. Business amenities include projector screen, voice and data access, ergonomic chairs, movable tables, break-out areas and complimentary beverages and ice.

The finest caterers are available upon request.

INNKEEPERS:	Kaye & David Caster
ADDRESS:	115 South 26th Street
	Colorado Springs, CO 80904
TELEPHONE:	(719) 632-9194
E-MAIL:	oldtown@rmi.net
WEBSITE:	www.oldtown-guesthouse.com
ROOMS:	8 Rooms; All with private baths
CHILDREN:	Children age 16 and older are welcome
ANIMALS:	Not allowed
HANDICAPPED:	Is handicapped accessible
DIETARY NEEDS:	Will accommodate guests' special dietary needs

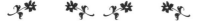

Old Town Chocolate Chip Pumpkin Bread

Makes 2 Loaves

Who could resist this pumpkin bread laced with chocolate chips? This recipe makes two loaves – enjoy one now and freeze the other for later.

3	cups all-purpose flour
2	teaspoons cinnamon
1	teaspoon salt
1	teaspoon baking soda
4	eggs
2	cups sugar
2	cups canned pumpkin
1¼	cups vegetable oil
1½	cups chocolate chips

Preheat oven to 350°F. Grease two 8x4-inch loaf pans. In a large bowl, sift together the flour, cinnamon, salt and baking soda. Make a well in the middle of the dry ingredients.

In another bowl, beat together the eggs, sugar, pumpkin and oil. Add the wet ingredients to the dry ingredients; stir just until moistened. Fold in the chocolate chips. Divide the batter equally between the two prepared pans.

Bake for 60-70 minutes, or until a toothpick inserted near the center of the loaves comes out clean. Cool the loaves in the pans for 10 minutes on a wire rack. Remove the bread from the pans and finish cooling on the rack.

Red Crags

R ed Crags Bed and Breakfast is a magnificent, four-story Victorian mansion known throughout the Pikes Peak area for over 120 years. The main house is 7,000 square feet and dominates the two acre estate.

Inside, guests marvel at the beautiful antiques, hardwood floors and high ceilings. The formal dining room, where a gourmet breakfast is served, features a rare cherry wood Eastlake fireplace.

INNKEEPERS:	Howard & Lynda Lerner
ADDRESS:	302 El Paso Boulevard
	Manitou Springs, CO 80829
TELEPHONE:	(719) 685-1920; (800) 721-2248
E-MAIL:	info@redcrags.com
WEBSITE:	www.redcrags.com
ROOMS:	3 Rooms; 5 Suites; All with private baths
CHILDREN:	Children age 10 and older are welcome
ANIMALS:	Not allowed
HANDICAPPED:	Not handicapped accessible
DIETARY NEEDS:	Will accommodate guests' special dietary needs

Pistachio Nut Bread

Makes 2 Loaves

This is a perfect treat for breakfast or with afternoon tea. If you cannot find pistachio oil, you can omit it and the bread will still be delicious and flavorful.

1   box yellow cake mix (without pudding in the mix)
1   (3.4-ounce) package instant pistachio pudding mix
3   drops pistachio oil (optional)
1   (8-ounce) carton sour cream
4   eggs, lightly beaten
¼   cup water
¼   cup vegetable oil
½   cup chopped pecans

Topping:
4   tablespoons sugar
2   teaspoons cinnamon

Preheat oven to 350°F. Grease two 9x5-inch loaf pans. In a large bowl, combine the cake mix, pudding mix, optional pistachio oil, sour cream, eggs, water, oil and pecans; mix well. Divide the batter between the two pans, reserving half of the batter for a second layer.

Make the topping by mixing together the sugar and cinnamon in a small bowl. Sprinkle half of the topping mixture evenly over the batter in the loaf pans. Using a knife, swirl the batter to lightly mix in some of the topping. Divide the remaining batter between the two pans. Sprinkle with the remaining topping; swirl lightly.

Bake loaves for 35-40 minutes. Let loaves cool in the pans on a wire rack for 10-15 minutes. Remove loaves and cool slightly on a wire rack to serve warm, or cool thoroughly to serve at room temperature.

Awarenest Victorian

The Awarenest Victorian Bed and Breakfast was built in 1901 for a conductor with the Denver-Rio Grande railway. It has been fully restored with authentic Victorian furnishings that include period antiques and vintage stained glass.

The inn is within walking distance of the quaint boutiques and charming eateries of Colorado Springs and the historic district of Old Colorado City.

INNKEEPERS:	Karla & Rex Hefferan
ADDRESS:	1218 West Pikes Peak Avenue
	Colorado Springs, CO 80904
TELEPHONE:	(719) 630-8241; (888) 910-8241
E-MAIL:	info@awarenest.com
WEBSITE:	www.awarenest.com
ROOMS:	1 Suite; Attached bath
CHILDREN:	Welcome
ANIMALS:	Not allowed; Resident pets
HANDICAPPED:	Not handicapped accessible
DIETARY NEEDS:	Will accommodate guests' special dietary needs

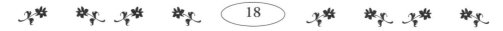

One Pan Banana Nut Bread

Makes 1 Loaf

⅓   cup vegetable oil
1½   cups mashed ripe bananas
½   teaspoon vanilla
3   eggs
2⅔   cups Bisquick
1   cup sugar
½   cup roughly chopped walnuts or pecans
½   cup chocolate chips (optional)

Preheat oven to 350°F. Mix all the ingredients together and bake in a greased 9x5-inch loaf pan for 55-65 minutes. Cool 5 minutes and remove from pan. Finish cooling on a wire rack.

Here in Colorado, follow high altitude adjustment as follows: Preheat oven to 375°F. Decrease Bisquick to 2 cups and sugar to ⅔ cup. Add ¼ cup all-purpose flour. Bake for 50-55 minutes.

> *Carol's Corner*
> *I tried this recipe adding the chocolate bits. The chocolate and banana flavors are a nice combination.*

Alps Boulder Canyon Inn

Located two miles west of Boulder, the Alps Boulder Canyon Inn is a turn-of-the-twentieth-century mountain lodge. Surrounded by the magnificent Rocky Mountains, this historic inn was once a stagecoach stop, bordello and lodge for miners traveling to and from Boulder County mines.

The large dining room features a moss rock fireplace. All rooms are decorated with family heirlooms and period antiques.

INNKEEPERS:	John & Jeannine Vanderhart
ADDRESS:	38619 Boulder Canyon Drive
	Boulder, CO 80302
TELEPHONE:	(303) 444-5445
E-MAIL:	info@alpsinn.com
WEBSITE:	www.alpsinn.com
ROOMS:	12 Rooms; All with private baths
CHILDREN:	Children age 12 and older are welcome
ANIMALS:	Not allowed; Resident dog
HANDICAPPED:	Not handicapped accessible
DIETARY NEEDS:	Will accommodate guests' special dietary needs

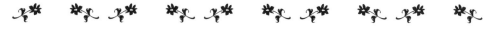

Alps Banana Nut Bread

Makes 1 Loaf

½   cup (1 stick) butter, room temperature
1   cup sugar
2   large eggs, beaten
4   medium-size ripe bananas, peeled and cut into ⅛-inch slices
2   cups all-purpose flour
1   teaspoon baking soda
1   teaspoon vanilla extract
½   cup chopped black walnuts

Preheat oven to 325°F. Grease and flour a 9x5-inch loaf pan. In a large bowl, beat together the butter and sugar. Add the beaten eggs and sliced bananas; mix well. Add the remaining ingredients; mix thoroughly (there will still be visible pieces of banana). Spoon the batter into the prepared loaf pan.

Bake for 60 minutes, or until a toothpick inserted in the middle of the loaf comes out clean. Cool on a wire rack for 15 minutes. Remove bread from pan and place on rack to finish cooling.

> ✽ *Carol's Corner*
> *To ripen a banana that is still slightly green, heat the unpeeled banana in the microwave for 30–60 seconds. Let the banana cool for 10 minutes or so, remove the peel and slice or mash for recipes.*

Old Town Guest House

B uilt in 1997, the Old Town Guest House is in perfect harmony with the 1859 period construction of Colorado Springs' historic old town. This elegant urban inn offers upscale amenities for discerning adults. The foyer has an elevator to facilitate access by all guests to all areas of the inn.

The eight guestrooms have been architecturally designed to offer maximum quiet, privacy, luxury, convenience and safety.

INNKEEPERS:	Kaye & David Caster
ADDRESS:	115 South 26th Street
	Colorado Springs, CO 80904
TELEPHONE:	(719) 632-9194
E-MAIL:	oldtown@rmi.net
WEBSITE:	www.oldtown-guesthouse.com
ROOMS:	8 Rooms; All with private baths
CHILDREN:	Children age 16 and older are welcome
ANIMALS:	Not allowed
HANDICAPPED:	Is handicapped accessible
DIETARY NEEDS:	Will accommodate guests' special dietary needs

Old Town Cranberry Bread

Makes 1 Loaf

Bake this very flavorful bread a day in advance, as it is best to refrigerate the loaf overnight before slicing and serving. This bread also freezes well.

1½	cups all-purpose flour
½	teaspoon salt
½	teaspoon cream of tartar
¼	teaspoon baking soda
½	cup chopped pecans
1	cup sugar
2	strips (about 3x1-inch each) lemon zest
½	cup (1 stick) unsalted butter, room temperature
2	eggs
¾	teaspoon vanilla extract
6	tablespoons plain yogurt
1½	cups fresh cranberries (or use dried cranberries, see *Carol's Corner*)

Preheat oven to 350°F. Grease and flour a 9x5-inch loaf pan. In a medium bowl, sift together flour, salt, cream of tartar and baking soda. Stir in pecans. In food processor, place sugar and lemon zest strips. Process until zest is finely grated. Add butter; process until creamy. Add eggs, one at a time; mix well. Add vanilla and yogurt; process until combined. Transfer butter/yogurt mixture to a large bowl.

Put cranberries in food processor; pulse 3 or 4 times until coarsely chopped. Add cranberries to dry ingredients; toss to combine. Add dry ingredients and cranberries to butter/yogurt mixture; stir just until moistened. Spoon batter into loaf pan. Bake for 50-60 minutes, or until a toothpick inserted in the center comes out clean. Cool on rack for 30 minutes. Remove bread from pan to finish cooling. Wrap well; refrigerate for 24 hours before serving.

> ⚘ *Carol's Corner*
> *I made this with a 6-ounce package of dried cranberries, soaked them in very hot water for 10 minutes and drained well. The dried cranberries worked great, and the bread was delicious!*

Last Dollar Inn

Located in historic Cripple Creek, the Last Dollar Inn Bed and Breakfast was built in 1898, two years after fires nearly destroyed the entire town. Built to house an office and residence, it also had rooms for rent.

After a extensive, recent renovation, the present owners offer guests a journey back in time during their stay at this beautifully restored Victorian bed and breakfast.

INNKEEPERS:	Rick & Janice Wood
ADDRESS:	315 East Carr Avenue
	Cripple Creek, CO 80813
TELEPHONE:	(719) 689-9113; (888) 429-6700
E-MAIL:	packy578@concentric.net
WEBSITE:	www.cripple-creek.co.us/lastdinn.htm
ROOMS:	6 Rooms; All with private baths
CHILDREN:	Not allowed
ANIMALS:	Not allowed
HANDICAPPED:	Not handicapped accessible
DIETARY NEEDS:	Will accommodate guests' special dietary needs

Corn Bread

Makes 9 Servings

"This is a down-home corn bread recipe with a sweet little twist created by a very curious cook one night. It has turned into a favorite for anyone who tastes it." — Rick & Janice Wood, Last Dollar Inn

1	cup cornmeal
1	cup all-purpose flour
½	cup sugar
4½	teaspoons baking powder
½	teaspoon salt
1	cup milk
1	egg
⅓	cup vegetable shortening
⅔	cup aerosol non-dairy whipped topping (or frozen whipped topping, such as Cool Whip, thawed)

Preheat oven to 425°F. Coat an 8x8-inch baking dish with nonstick cooking spray. In a large bowl, mix together the corn meal, flour, sugar, baking powder and salt. Add the milk, egg and shortening. Beat well until fairly smooth, about 1 minute. Fold in the whipped topping. Spoon the batter into the prepared baking dish.

Bake for 20-25 minutes, or until a toothpick inserted in the center comes out clean. Serve hot, with butter.

Blue Skies

Nestled at the base of Pikes Peak, the Blue Skies Inn is located in Manitou Springs, a scenic mountain town founded in 1873 by Dr. William Bell. Dr. Bell established a health resort centered around the town's many artesian mineral springs.

The three buildings that comprise the Blue Skies Inn are clustered around Dr. Bell's original carriage house.

INNKEEPERS:	Sally & Mike
ADDRESS:	402 Manitou Avenue
	Manitou Springs, CO 80829
TELEPHONE:	(719) 685-3899; (800) 398-7949
E-MAIL:	sally@blueskiesbb.com
WEBSITE:	www.blueskiesbb.com
ROOMS:	10 Suites; All with private baths
CHILDREN:	Welcome
ANIMALS:	Not allowed
HANDICAPPED:	Is handicapped accessible
DIETARY NEEDS:	Will accommodate guests' special dietary needs

Sunny Skies Muffins

Makes 12 Muffins

2½ cups all-purpose flour
½   cup sugar
1   tablespoon baking powder
½   teaspoon salt
1   egg
1   cup milk
¼   cup (½ stick) butter, melted
1   cup fresh blueberries
Sugar for tops of muffins (optional)

Preheat oven to 375°F. Coat 12 muffin cups with nonstick cooking spray, or use paper liners. In a large bowl, sift together the flour, sugar, baking powder and salt. Make a well in the center of the dry ingredients.

In a small bowl, beat together the egg and milk. Add the melted butter; mix well. Add the wet ingredients to the dry ingredients. Stir just until moistened. Gently fold in the blueberries.

Spoon the batter into the prepared muffin cups, filling each almost full.

Optional: For an added touch of sweetness and sparkle, sugar may be sprinkled on top of the batter before baking.

Bake for 20-25 minutes, or until muffins are golden. Cool in muffin cups on a wire rack for 5 minutes. Remove from muffin cups; serve warm.

Cattail Creek

Designed and built as a luxury inn, the Cattail Creek Inn Bed and Breakfast is a perfect destination for both leisure and business travelers. Located on the seventh tee of Cattail Golf Course, this elegant inn is within walking distance of Benson Sculpture Park.

Bountiful breakfasts feature homemade breads and scones, Rocky Mountain French toast, artichoke bacon frittata and homemade granola.

INNKEEPERS:	Sue & Harold Buchman
ADDRESS:	2665 Abarr Drive
	Loveland, CO 80538
TELEPHONE:	(970) 667-7600; (800) 572-2466
E-MAIL:	info@cattailcreekinn.com
WEBSITE:	www.cattailcreekinn.com
ROOMS:	8 Rooms; All with private baths
CHILDREN:	Children age 14 and older are welcome
ANIMALS:	Not allowed
HANDICAPPED:	Is handicapped accessible
DIETARY NEEDS:	Will accommodate guests' special dietary needs

Apricot Pecan Muffins

Makes 12 Muffins

These muffins are crunchy on top and moist inside – perfection!

1	cup dried apricots, chopped
1	cup boiling water
1	cup sugar
½	cup (1 stick) butter, room temperature
1	cup sour cream
2	cups all-purpose flour
1	teaspoon baking soda
½	teaspoon salt
1	tablespoon grated orange zest
½	cup chopped pecans

Preheat oven to 400°F. Grease 12 muffin cups, or use paper liners. Soak chopped apricots in boiling water for 5 minutes. In a large bowl, cream the sugar and butter together until fluffy. Add the sour cream; mix well.

In a medium bowl, sift together the flour, baking soda and salt. Stir the dry ingredients into the creamed mixture; stir just until moistened. Drain the apricots, discarding the liquid. Fold apricots, orange zest and pecans into the batter (batter will be stiff). Fill the prepared muffin cups about ¾ full.

Bake for 18-20 minutes, or until the muffins test done. Watch the muffins closely because they can burn easily. Cool the muffins in the pan for 10 minutes on a wire rack. Remove the muffins; serve warm.

Chipita Park

Chipita Lodge

Located at the base of Pikes Peak, the Chipita Lodge Bed and Breakfast was built in 1927 of native log and stone. This historic lodge has served as a general store, post office, community center and land development office. Additional buildings on the property include a stone structure that housed Chipita Park's first fire truck and the remains of an icehouse where ice from Chipita Lake was stored for later transport to Colorado Springs.

Guests are treated to a full breakfast either in the lodge or on the deck.

INNKEEPERS:	Kevin & Martha Henry
ADDRESS:	9090 Chipita Park Road
	Chipita Park, CO 80809
TELEPHONE:	(719) 684-8454
E-MAIL:	chipitainn@aol.com
WEBSITE:	www.chipitalodge.com
ROOMS:	3 Rooms; 2 Cottages; All with private baths
CHILDREN:	Welcome (Cottages only)
ANIMALS:	Dogs welcome (Cottages only); Resident dog
HANDICAPPED:	Not handicapped accessible
DIETARY NEEDS:	Will accommodate guests' special dietary needs

Sunshine Muffins

Makes 12 Muffins

A blender is a necessary piece of equipment to make these muffins that have such intriguing recipe directions.

1	orange (any kind)
½	cup orange juice
1	egg
¼	cup vegetable oil
1½	cups flour
¾	cup sugar
1	teaspoon baking powder
1	teaspoon baking soda
1	teaspoon salt
½	cup raisins (optional)
½	cup chopped nuts

Preheat oven to 375°F. Coat a 12-count muffin tin with nonstick cooking spray, or use paper liners. Wash the orange and cut it into 8 pieces. Put the orange pieces (yup, the peel, the seeds – the whole thing), orange juice, egg and oil into a blender. Process until smooth.

In a large bowl, sift together the flour, sugar, baking powder, baking soda and salt. Make a well in the middle of the dry ingredients. Add the blender mixture to the dry ingredients, then the raisins and nuts. Mix just until moistened. Spoon the batter into muffin tins, filling the cups about ¾ full.

Bake for 15-20 minutes, or until muffins are golden.

The Queen Anne

Elegance and history converge in the two, side-by-side Victorian houses in downtown Denver that comprise The Queen Anne Bed and Breakfast Inn. Special features include a grand oak staircase, rare 35-foot turret, antiques, art and flowers that showcase the warm hospitality for which the West, Denver and this inn are well known.

The Queen Anne was the first bed and breakfast inn in the city of Denver.

INNKEEPERS:	The King Family
ADDRESS:	2147-51 Tremont Place, Denver, CO 80205
TELEPHONE:	(303) 296-6666; (800) 432-INNS
E-MAIL:	travel@queenannebnb.com
WEBSITE:	www.queenannebnb.com
ROOMS:	4 Two-Bedroom Suites; 10 Double Rooms; All with private baths
CHILDREN:	Welcome
ANIMALS:	Not allowed
HANDICAPPED:	Not handicapped accessible
DIETARY NEEDS:	Will accommodate guests' special dietary needs

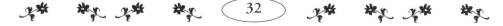

Lemony Orange Muffins

Makes 24 Muffins

1	cup sugar
⅔	cup shortening
2	eggs
2	tablespoons fresh lemon juice
3	cups all-purpose flour
1	tablespoon baking powder
½	teaspoon salt
1	teaspoon nutmeg
1	cup milk

Orange glaze (recipe below)
Orange butter (recipe below)

Preheat oven to 350°F. Coat a muffin tin with nonstick cooking spray, or use paper liners. In a large bowl, cream together sugar, shortening, eggs and lemon juice. Sift together flour, baking powder, salt and nutmeg. Add to creamed mixture alternately with milk. Stir with spoon – do not overmix. Fill muffin tins ½ to ⅔ full. Bake for 20-25 minutes. Brush muffins with Orange Glaze while still warm. Let muffins cool. Serve with Orange Butter.

Orange glaze:

1½	cups powdered sugar
3-4	tablespoons freshly squeezed orange juice
2	tablespoons grated orange zest

Combine all ingredients in a medium bowl.

Orange butter:

3	tablespoons powdered sugar
2	tablespoons grated orange zest
½	cup (1 stick) unsalted butter, softened

Combine all ingredients in a small bowl.

Derby Hill Inn

Located in a quiet neighborhood on the south side of Loveland, in northern Colorado, the Derby Hill Inn Bed and Breakfast features rooms accented with country ambiance and beautiful antiques. Breakfast is served in a formal dining room or on a unique glass-covered redwood deck.

"The friendliness, service and food make this what hospitality is all about."
— Guest, Derby Hill B & B

INNKEEPERS:	Dale & Bev McCue
ADDRESS:	2502 Courtney Drive
	Loveland, CO 80537
TELEPHONE:	(970) 667-3193
E-MAIL:	dmccue31@aol.com
WEBSITE:	www.bbonline.com/co/derbyhill
ROOMS:	2 Rooms; Both with private baths
CHILDREN:	Children age 12 and older are welcome
ANIMALS:	Not allowed
HANDICAPPED:	Not handicapped accessible
DIETARY NEEDS:	Will accommodate guests' special dietary needs

Morning Glory Muffins

Makes 12 to 18 Muffins

"Sucanant is a sweetener that can be purchased at natural food stores. It is a blend of molasses and evaporated cane juice. We like the molasses flavor it adds to these muffins. This recipe is a favorite of our guests." — Dale & Bev McCue, Derby Hill Inn B&B. These muffins freeze well – keep some in the freezer for handy, healthy snacks.

1   cup golden raisins
Hot water to soak raisins
2   cups unbleached flour
1   cup sugar or sucanant (see innkeeper's note above)
2   teaspoons baking soda
2   teaspoons cinnamon
½   teaspoon salt
2   cups grated carrot
1   tart green apple, peeled and diced
½   cup sliced almonds
½   cup shredded coconut
3   eggs
⅔   cup butter, melted and cooled
2   teaspoons pure vanilla extract

Preheat oven to 350°F. Cover raisins with hot water and let soak for 20-30 minutes; drain well. Grease muffins cups, or use paper liners. In a large bowl, sift together the flour, sugar (or sucanant), baking soda, cinnamon and salt. Add drained raisins, carrots, apple, almonds and coconut; stir to combine. In a small bowl, whisk together the eggs, butter and vanilla. Add the egg mixture to the flour mixture; stir just enough to blend together – do not overmix.

Spoon the batter into muffin cups, filling cups about ¾ full. Bake 20-25 minutes, or until muffins are done. Let cool in pan a few minutes. Remove muffins from muffin cups and serve or place on a cooling rack.

Wild Horse Inn

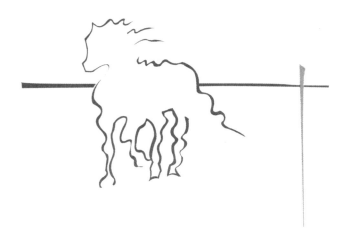

Handcrafted from 400-year-old Engelmann spruce logs, moss covered rock and giant picture windows, the Wild Horse Inn is reminiscent of the grand mountain lodges built at the turn of the twentieth century. Located just 90 minutes from Denver, this inviting inn sits nestled among acres of trees and meadows on a ridge above the Fraser Valley.

Guests are minutes from skiing, biking, fly-fishing, rafting or hiking.

INNKEEPERS:	John Cribari & Christine French
ADDRESS:	1536 County Road 83
	Fraser, CO 80442
TELEPHONE:	(970) 726-0456
E-MAIL:	info@wildhorseinncolorado.com
WEBSITE:	www.wildhorseinncolorado.com
ROOMS:	7 Rooms; All with private baths
CHILDREN:	Not allowed
ANIMALS:	Not allowed
HANDICAPPED:	Not handicapped accessible
DIETARY NEEDS:	Will accommodate guests' special dietary needs

Strawberry & Cream Muffins

Makes 12 Muffins

"We love to serve these muffins with butter, raspberry jam and a side of whole strawberries." — Christine French & John Cribari, Wild Horse Inn

½   cup (1 stick) butter, room temperature
1   cup sugar
2   large eggs, beaten
½   cup sour cream
2   teaspoons vanilla extract
1⅔   cups all-purpose flour
2   teaspoons baking powder
1   cup chopped fresh strawberries

Preheat oven to 375°F. Grease the cups of a muffin tin, or use paper liners. In a large bowl, cream the butter and sugar. Add the beaten eggs, sour cream and vanilla.

Sift the flour and baking powder together; gradually stir into the wet ingredients. Gently fold in the strawberries. The dough will be somewhat stiff. Do not overmix, or the muffins will be tough. Spoon the batter into the muffin cups.

Bake for about 20 minutes, or until the tops of the muffins are lightly springy and slightly brown. Let cool for 5 minutes before turning the muffins out onto a wire rack.

Stone Mansion

The historic Stone Mansion Bed and Breakfast is a unique example of early twentieth-century aesthetic sensibility. Built in 1904, this grand mansion is beautifully preserved. The interior is expansive and contains many classical elements including original quarter-sawn golden oak woodwork and museum-quality oil paintings, furniture and family heirlooms.

A sumptuous gourmet breakfast is served in the lavish dining room.

INNKEEPERS:	Robert & Jane Barker
ADDRESS:	212 East 2nd Street
	Trinidad, CO 81082
TELEPHONE:	(719) 845-1625
E-MAIL:	Not available
WEBSITE:	Not available
ROOMS:	3 Rooms; 1 Private and 1 shared bath
CHILDREN:	Children age 8 and older are welcome
ANIMALS:	Dogs welcome (call ahead); Resident cats
HANDICAPPED:	Not handicapped accessible
DIETARY NEEDS:	Will accommodate guests' special dietary needs

Chocolate Muffins

Makes 12 to 18 Muffins

Need some chocolate to start your day? Give these double-dosed muffins a try!

1½	cups all-purpose flour
½	cup unsweetened cocoa powder
2	teaspoons baking powder
¼	teaspoon salt
¼	cup (½ stick) butter
⅓	cup plus 1 tablespoon sugar (or more for sweeter muffins)
2	eggs
¾	cup milk
1	teaspoon vanilla extract
½	cup chocolate chips

Powdered sugar for dusting (optional)

Preheat oven to 425°F. Grease muffin tins, or use paper liners. In a large bowl, sift together the flour, cocoa, baking powder and salt. Make a well in the middle of the dry mixture. In a medium, microwaveable bowl, melt butter with all the sugar in the microwave (about 30-45 seconds). Beat in the eggs, milk and vanilla. Add the wet ingredients to the dry ingredients and mix just until moistened. Stir in the chocolate chips. Do not overmix.

Spoon the batter into the muffin cups ½ to ¾ full. Bake for about 15 minutes, or until lightly browned. Remove muffins quickly from the muffin cups after baking. Dust with powdered sugar, if desired. Muffins are best served hot-out-of-the-oven with fresh butter.

Note: Muffins can be baked in mini-muffin cups … perfect for teatime. Shorten baking time accordingly.

Steamboat Valley Guest House

Built on Crawford Hill in 1957 with logs from the town mill and bricks from the old flour mill, Steamboat Valley Guest House was the Yampa Valley College president's residence in the 1960's. It was remodeled as a bed and breakfast in 1993.

The Guest House is within easy walking distance of Old Town shops and restaurants, and features ski and bike storage and an outdoor hot tub.

INNKEEPERS:	Alice & George Lund
ADDRESS:	1245 Crawford Avenue; PO Box 773815
	Steamboat Springs, CO 80477
TELEPHONE:	(970) 870-9017; (800) 530-3866
E-MAIL:	george@steamboatvalley.com
WEBSITE:	www.steamboatvalley.com
ROOMS:	3 Rooms; 1 Suite; All with private baths
CHILDREN:	Not allowed
ANIMALS:	Not allowed
HANDICAPPED:	Not handicapped accessible
DIETARY NEEDS:	Call ahead

Ice Box English Tea Muffins

Makes 12 Muffins

½   cup (1 stick) butter
¾   cup sugar
1   egg
½   teaspoon salt
¼   teaspoon cinnamon
2   teaspoons baking powder
2   cups flour
1   cup milk
¾   cup currants

Topping:
½   cup brown sugar
¼   cup chopped pecans
1   teaspoon cinnamon

Preheat oven to 350°F. In a large bowl, cream butter and sugar together. Add egg and blend well. In a separate bowl, combine salt, cinnamon, baking powder and flour; add alternately with milk to the creamed mixture. Stir in currants.

Spoon into greased muffin cups about ¾ full. Combine topping ingredients and sprinkle on muffins. Press topping in slightly. Bake for 20-25 minutes.

Make-ahead tip: Batter may be covered tightly and stored in refrigerator for 2-3 weeks.

Thomas House

The Thomas House Bed and Breakfast was built in 1888 as a rooming house for the travelers and businesspeople brought by the Denver and Rio Grande Railroad. Railroad workers flocked to Salida, which became a major intersection for narrow and standard gauge rail.

Driving into Salida, a sign reads, "Now this is Colorado." With more warmth and sunshine, more world famous river rapids and more 14,000 foot peaks than any other Colorado county, this is certainly not an overstatement.

INNKEEPERS:	Tammy & Steve Office
ADDRESS:	307 East First Street
	Salida, CO 81201
TELEPHONE:	(719) 539-7104
EMAIL:	office@thomashouse.com
WEBSITE:	www.thomashouse.com
ROOMS:	4 rooms; 1 Suite; 1 Cottage; All with private baths
CHILDREN:	Welcome
ANIMALS:	Not allowed
HANDICAPPED:	Not Accessible
DIETARY NEEDS:	Will accommodate guests' special dietary needs

Six-Week Raisin Bran Muffins

Makes 24 Muffins

"This recipe has been a savior when dealing with an especially large or small (more than 12 or less than 4) breakfast crowd. You don't have to think very clearly in the morning to get great results every time, and you can make only the number of muffins you need, so there is little waste." — Tammy Office, Thomas House B&B

2½   cups flour
2½   teaspoons baking soda
1   teaspoon salt
½   teaspoon cinnamon
¼   teaspoon allspice
1½   cups sugar
3   cups (6 ounces) Raisin Bran cereal
2   cups buttermilk
2   eggs, beaten
½   cup vegetable oil

Topping:
½   cup sugar
½   teaspoon cinnamon

In a very large bowl, mix together the flour, baking soda, salt, spices, sugar and cereal. Add buttermilk, eggs and oil. Mix thoroughly.

Make-ahead tip: At this point, you may transfer the batter to a large air-tight container and refrigerate for up to 6 weeks.

When ready to bake, preheat oven to 375°F. Fill greased and floured muffin cups ¾ full and bake 20-25 minutes, or until a toothpick comes out clean. Combine the topping ingredients in a small bowl. Remove muffins from pan immediately and dip the tops of the muffins into the cinnamon-sugar mixture. Best when served warm.

Elizabeth Street Guest House

Elizabeth Street Guest House is a beautifully restored, American Four-square brick home, lovingly furnished with family antiques, old quilts and handmade crafts. The leaded windows and oak woodwork are special features, as is the unique three-story miniature house in the entry hall.

Located in the historic heart of Fort Collins, Elizabeth Street Guest House is one block east of Colorado State University.

INNKEEPERS:	John & Sheryl Clark
ADDRESS:	202 East Elizabeth Street
	Ft. Collins, CO 80524
TELEPHONE:	(970) 493-BEDS
E-MAIL:	sheryl.clark@juno.com
WEBSITE:	www.bbonline.com/co/elizabeth
ROOMS:	3 Rooms; Private & shared baths
CHILDREN:	Not allowed
ANIMALS:	Not allowed; Resident dog
HANDICAPPED:	Not handicapped accessible
DIETARY NEEDS:	Will accommodate guests' special dietary needs

Raisin-Oatmeal Muffins

Makes 12 Muffins

1	cup raisins
2	tablespoons apple juice or water
¾	cup flour
2	teaspoons baking powder
¾	teaspoon salt
⅓	cup sugar
1	cup rolled oats (not instant oats)
2	eggs
½	cup milk
¼	cup vegetable oil

Topping:

2	tablespoons ground nuts, such as walnuts or pecans
2	tablespoons sugar
1	teaspoon cinnamon

Preheat oven to 400°F. Coat muffin pans with nonstick cooking spray, or use paper liners.

Sprinkle raisins with apple juice (or water) and microwave for 30 seconds. Set aside to cool.

In a large bowl, stir flour, baking powder, salt and sugar together thoroughly. Stir in oats and raisins (including juice). In a small bowl, combine eggs, milk and oil. Beat well with fork. Add wet ingredients to dry ingredients and stir just until moistened.

Fill muffin cups about ⅔ full. Combine topping ingredients and sprinkle onto muffins. Bake for 15-20 minutes, or until top of muffins springs back when lightly touched.

Coffee Cakes,
Biscuits,
Rolls &
Scones

Leadville Country Inn

Located at 10,200 feet, the Leadville Country Inn is a stately 15 room Queen Anne Victorian constructed in 1892 by Herbert Demick, an architect and builder who favored majestic homes with towers, rounded porches and grand staircases.

Acclaimed for its mining history, the Leadville of 1892, was a booming mountain city with a population of 40,000 hardy pioneers and miners, that epitomized all that was bold and exciting about Colorado's early days.

INNKEEPERS:	Maureen & Gretchen Scanlon
ADDRESS:	127 East 8th Street
	Leadville, CO 80461
TELEPHONE:	(719) 486-2354
E-MAIL:	lcinn@bemail.com
WEBSITE:	www.leadvillebednbreakfast.com
ROOMS:	8 Rooms; All with private baths
CHILDREN:	Children age 10 and older are welcome
ANIMALS:	Not allowed
HANDICAPPED:	Not handicapped accessible
DIETARY NEEDS:	Will accommodate guests' special dietary needs

Oatmeal Coffee Cake

Makes 12 to 15 Servings

This cake is moist and flavorful. The recipe can be halved and baked in an 11x7-inch baking pan. It can also be baked ahead of time and frozen. Option: For a toasted coconut look and taste (sweet, nutty and crunchy), remove cake from the oven after 30 minutes. Spread the topping on the cake and return to the oven for 5-7 minutes, until cake is done and coconut is lightly browned.

1¼	cups boiling water
1	cup rolled oats (not instant oats)
½	cup (1 stick) butter, cut into several pieces
1	cup sugar
1	cup packed brown sugar
1½	cups all-purpose flour
1	teaspoon cinnamon
1	teaspoon baking powder
1	teaspoon baking soda
½	teaspoon salt
½	cup chopped walnuts
2	eggs, lightly beaten
1	teaspoon vanilla extract

Topping:

¼	cup milk
½	cup sugar
¼	cup chopped walnuts
1½	cups shredded coconut
½	teaspoon vanilla extract
¼	cup (½ stick) butter, melted

Preheat oven to 350°F. Grease a 13x9-inch baking pan. In a large bowl, combine boiling water, oats and butter. Let mixture stand until the butter is melted, stirring occasionally. In a medium bowl, combine sugar, brown sugar, flour, cinnamon, baking powder, baking soda, salt and nuts. Add the dry mixture to the oatmeal mixture, along with eggs and vanilla. Mix well. Pour the batter into the baking pan. Bake for 35 minutes, until done. Meanwhile, combine the topping ingredients. When the cake is done, spread the topping over hot cake. Cool on a wire rack before serving.

Derby Hill Inn

S et amidst an eclectic art collection, sculpture and interesting accents, the sitting room of the Derby Hill Inn Bed and Breakfast has a character all its own, where guests can be found relaxing or reading on the comfortable furniture, including a love seat rocker.

"Most relaxing to those of us who have to conduct business on the road. You made a great contribution to the success of our show." — Guest, Derby Hill B & B

INNKEEPERS:	Dale & Bev McCue
ADDRESS:	2502 Courtney Drive
	Loveland, CO 80537
TELEPHONE:	(970) 667-3193
E-MAIL:	dmccue31@aol.com
WEBSITE:	www.bbonline.com/co/derbyhill
ROOMS:	2 Rooms; Both have private baths
CHILDREN:	Children age 12 and older are welcome
ANIMALS:	Not allowed
HANDICAPPED:	Not handicapped accessible
DIETARY NEEDS:	Will accommodate guests' special dietary needs

Raspberry Almond Coffee Cake

Makes 6 to 8 Servings

1	cup fresh raspberries
1	tablespoon brown sugar
1	cup all-purpose flour
⅓	cup sugar
½	teaspoon baking powder
¼	teaspoon baking soda
⅛	teaspoon salt
½	cup plain low-fat yogurt
2	tablespoons butter, melted
1	teaspoon vanilla extract
1	large egg
1	tablespoon sliced almonds
¼	cup powdered sugar, sifted
1	teaspoon skim milk
¼	teaspoon almond extract

Preheat oven to 350°F. Coat an 8-inch round cake pan with nonstick cooking spray. In a small bowl, combine the raspberries and brown sugar. In a large bowl, sift together the flour, sugar, baking powder, baking soda and salt. In a small bowl, combine the yogurt, melted butter, vanilla and egg. Add the yogurt mixture to the flour mixture, stirring until just moistened.

Spoon ⅔ of the batter into the pan; spread evenly. Top with the raspberry mixture, spreading it to within ½-inch of the edge of the pan. Spoon the remaining batter by small spoonfuls, over the raspberry mixture. (The batter will not completely cover the raspberries.) Top with the almonds.

Bake for 30-40 minutes, or until the top is golden and a toothpick inserted in the center comes out clean. Let cool 10 minutes on a wire rack.

Make a glaze by combining powdered sugar, milk and almond extract; stir until smooth. If necessary, add a few more drops of milk to make a drizzling consistency. Drizzle the glaze over the cake. Cut into wedges and serve warm or at room temperature.

Inn on Mapleton Hill

Carefully restored to preserve its character and charm, the Inn on Mapleton Hill offers individually decorated guestrooms and several distinctive and comfortable sitting areas. The antique furnishings include four-poster beds, artwork, armoires, sofas, desks, mirrors and claw foot tubs fitted with showers. Some rooms also have fireplaces.

Breakfast features fresh fruit, homemade baked goods, granola, cinnamon French toast and eggs with cheese and herbs.

INNKEEPERS:	Judi & Ray Schultze
ADDRESS:	1001 Spruce Street
	Boulder, CO 80302
TELEPHONE:	(303) 449-6528
E-MAIL:	maphillinn@aol.com
WEBSITE:	www.innonmapletonhill.com
ROOMS:	7 Rooms; 2 Suites; Private & shared baths
CHILDREN:	Children age 12 and older are welcome
ANIMALS:	Not allowed
HANDICAPPED:	Not handicapped accessible
DIETARY NEEDS:	Will accommodate guests' special dietary needs

Raspberry Almond Coffee Cake

Makes 6 to 8 Servings

1	cup fresh raspberries
1	tablespoon brown sugar
1	cup all-purpose flour
⅓	cup sugar
½	teaspoon baking powder
¼	teaspoon baking soda
⅛	teaspoon salt
½	cup plain low-fat yogurt
2	tablespoons butter, melted
1	teaspoon vanilla extract
1	large egg
1	tablespoon sliced almonds
¼	cup powdered sugar, sifted
1	teaspoon skim milk
¼	teaspoon almond extract

Preheat oven to 350°F. Coat an 8-inch round cake pan with nonstick cooking spray. In a small bowl, combine the raspberries and brown sugar. In a large bowl, sift together the flour, sugar, baking powder, baking soda and salt. In a small bowl, combine the yogurt, melted butter, vanilla and egg. Add the yogurt mixture to the flour mixture, stirring until just moistened.

Spoon ⅔ of the batter into the pan; spread evenly. Top with the raspberry mixture, spreading it to within ½-inch of the edge of the pan. Spoon the remaining batter by small spoonfuls, over the raspberry mixture. (The batter will not completely cover the raspberries.) Top with the almonds.

Bake for 30-40 minutes, or until the top is golden and a toothpick inserted in the center comes out clean. Let cool 10 minutes on a wire rack.

Make a glaze by combining powdered sugar, milk and almond extract; stir until smooth. If necessary, add a few more drops of milk to make a drizzling consistency. Drizzle the glaze over the cake. Cut into wedges and serve warm or at room temperature.

Inn on Mapleton Hill

Carefully restored to preserve its character and charm, the Inn on Mapleton Hill offers individually decorated guestrooms and several distinctive and comfortable sitting areas. The antique furnishings include four-poster beds, artwork, armoires, sofas, desks, mirrors and claw foot tubs fitted with showers. Some rooms also have fireplaces.

Breakfast features fresh fruit, homemade baked goods, granola, cinnamon French toast and eggs with cheese and herbs.

INNKEEPERS:	Judi & Ray Schultze
ADDRESS:	1001 Spruce Street
	Boulder, CO 80302
TELEPHONE:	(303) 449-6528
E-MAIL:	maphillinn@aol.com
WEBSITE:	www.innonmapletonhill.com
ROOMS:	7 Rooms; 2 Suites; Private & shared baths
CHILDREN:	Children age 12 and older are welcome
ANIMALS:	Not allowed
HANDICAPPED:	Not handicapped accessible
DIETARY NEEDS:	Will accommodate guests' special dietary needs

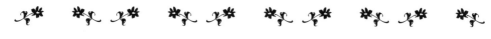

Judi's Chocolate Cinnamon Swirl Cake

Makes 12 Servings

A treat to top off breakfast on a Sunday morning!

1   cup (2 sticks) butter, room temperature
1   (8-ounce) package cream cheese, room temperature
1½   cups sugar
1½   teaspoons pure vanilla extract
4   eggs, beaten
2¼   cups all-purpose flour
1½   teaspoons baking powder
1   cup semi-sweet chocolate chips

Topping:
½   cup sugar
2   tablespoons cinnamon
5   teaspoons unsweetened cocoa powder

Preheat oven to 325°F. Coat a 13x9-inch glass baking dish with nonstick cooking spray. In a large bowl, blend butter and cream cheese. Add sugar and vanilla; mix well. Add beaten eggs; blend well. Add flour and baking powder; mix thoroughly. Stir in chocolate chips. Spread half of the batter into the prepared baking dish.

In a small bowl, mix together the topping ingredients. Sprinkle half of the topping mixture evenly over the batter in the baking dish (do not swirl). Drop the remaining batter by small spoonfuls over the first layer of batter. Gently spread to evenly cover. Sprinkle the remaining topping mixture over the batter (do not swirl).

Bake for 45 minutes, or until a toothpick inserted in the center comes out clean. Serve warm.

Leadville Country Inn

L ocated in historic Leadville, the Leadville Country Inn is a beautifully restored Victorian bed and breakfast. Renowned for its peaceful setting, this grand home is the perfect setting for a romantic getaway.

Leadville, the highest incorporated city in America, is situated in the very heart of Colorado's Rocky Mountains and offers myriad activities in a breathtaking setting of natural beauty, surrounded by 14,000-foot peaks.

INNKEEPERS:	Maureen & Gretchen Scanlon
ADDRESS:	127 East 8th Street
	Leadville, CO 80461
TELEPHONE:	(719) 486-2354
E-MAIL:	lcinn@bemail.com
WEBSITE:	www.leadvillebednbreakfast.com
ROOMS:	8 Rooms; All with private baths
CHILDREN:	Children age 10 and older are welcome
ANIMALS:	Not allowed
HANDICAPPED:	Not handicapped accessible
DIETARY NEEDS:	Will accommodate guests' special dietary needs

Lemon Breakfast Cake

Makes 8 Servings

1½   cups flour
1   cup sugar
1   teaspoon baking powder
½   teaspoon salt
2   eggs
½   cup milk
½   cup vegetable oil
Grated zest of 1 lemon
Lemon glaze (recipe below)
Powdered sugar for dusting
Lemon slices for garnish

Preheat oven to 350°F. Coat an 11x7-inch baking dish with nonstick cooking spray. In a large bowl, sift together the flour, sugar, baking powder and salt. Make a well in the middle of the dry ingredients. In a medium bowl, beat together the eggs, milk, oil and lemon zest. Add the wet ingredients to the dry ingredients. Stir until mixed.

Pour the batter into the prepared baking dish. Bake for approximately 30 minutes. When the cake is almost done, prepare the glaze.

When the cake is done, remove from the oven and, using a toothpick or an ice pick, poke holes in the top of the cake all the way to the bottom. Slowly drizzle the hot glaze over the top of the cake. Let the cake sit for 10 minutes. Dust each serving with powdered sugar and garnish with a lemon slice. The cake is best served warm, but is also good at room temperature.

Lemon glaze:
Juice of 1 lemon
⅓   cup sugar

Make the lemon glaze by combining the lemon juice and sugar in a small saucepan. Stir over low heat until the sugar dissolves.

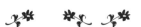

Alpen Rose

Hidden away just minutes from downtown Winter Park, the Alpen Rose Bed and Breakfast boasts of "Austrian warmth and hospitality." A large deck off the lodge's common room affords a panoramic view, highlighted by the western side of the majestic Front Range.

Each of the four bedrooms is exquisitely decorated with treasures brought from Austria, including traditional featherbeds.

INNKEEPERS:	Robin & Rupert Sommerauer
ADDRESS:	244 Forest Trail; PO Box 769
	Winter Park, CO 80482
TELEPHONE:	(970) 726-5039; (866) 531-1373
E-MAIL:	Not available
WEBSITE:	Not available
ROOMS:	8 Rooms; Private & shared baths
CHILDREN:	Welcome
ANIMALS:	Not allowed
HANDICAPPED:	Not handicapped accessible
DIETARY NEEDS:	Cannot accommodate guests' special dietary needs

Austrian Apple Strudel

Makes 4 to 6 Servings

"I like to prepare the strudel in advance and freeze until baking time. It's a favorite at the breakfast table and is also wonderful in the afternoon with tea or coffee." — Robin Sommerauer, Alpen Rose B&B

1   sheet frozen puff pastry (Pepperidge Farm recommended)
1   large green apple, such as Granny Smith
2-3   tablespoons butter
⅓-½ cup golden raisins
8-10 dried apricot halves, cut in quarters
¼   cup water
¼   cup packed light brown sugar
½   teaspoon cinnamon
¼   teaspoon nutmeg
1   egg yolk beaten with 1 tablespoon water

Thaw puff pastry. Cut and core apple and chop into ½-inch pieces. Over medium heat, melt butter in a large skillet. Add apple, raisins and apricots. Mix well and sauté for a few minutes. Add water, brown sugar, cinnamon and nutmeg. Cover and simmer for about 10 minutes. Cool.

Place pastry on a flat surface and distribute apple mixture down the middle of pastry sheet. Make 2½-inch long cuts diagonally along both sides of exposed pastry at 1½-inch intervals. Fold strips over apples alternating from left to right. Press dough together where ends overlap. With fork tines, seal top and bottom edge of dough. At this point, refrigerate for 30 minutes, or wrap and freeze for later use.

Preheat oven to 425°F. At time of baking, place strudel on a cookie sheet covered with parchment paper, or use an insulated cookie sheet to prevent overbrowning of the bottom of the pastry. Brush with the egg/water mixture (egg wash). Bake for 25 minutes, or until light golden brown.

Plum House

Plum House Bed and Breakfast is located in Red Cliff, a block from the spectacular Shrine Pass. The owner, Sydney Summers, is an artist, gallery owner and gourmet cook. She will prepare dinner with 24-hour notice.

Breakfasts include homemade muffins, rolls and a variety of other delectable treats. Guests enjoy the hot tub after a day of skiing or hiking, or just lounge in the living room by the wood stove.

INNKEEPERS:	Sydney Summers
ADDRESS:	236 Eagle Street; PO Box 41
	Red Cliff, CO 81649
TELEPHONE:	(970) 827-5881
E-MAIL:	sydney@mountainmax.net
WEBSITE:	None
ROOMS:	1 Room; Private bath
CHILDREN:	Not allowed
ANIMALS:	Not allowed
HANDICAPPED:	Not handicapped accessible
DIETARY NEEDS:	Will accommodate guests' special dietary needs

Best Biscuits

Makes 10 Biscuits

"These are old-fashioned biscuits and wonderful with my homemade jellies and preserves. Delicious!" — Sydney Summers, Plum House B&B

2	cups all-purpose flour
4	teaspoons baking powder
½	teaspoon salt
½	teaspoon cream of tartar
2	teaspoons sugar
½	cup shortening (butter flavored Crisco is best)
⅔	cup milk

Preheat oven to 450°F. In a medium bowl, sift together dry ingredients. Cut in shortening until it resembles coarse crumbs. Mix in milk and stir just until dough is moistened.

Turn out on a floured board and knead about 30 seconds. Flatten to about ¾-inch thick and cut with a glass dipped in flour. Place biscuits on an ungreased cookie sheet. Bake for 10-13 minutes, until lightly browned.

Barbara's

B arbara's Bed and Breakfast is nestled on Little Prospect Mountain in Estes Park. While sitting on the deck, guests enjoy beautiful scenery and may catch a glimpse of the variety of wildlife.

A quaint antique and gift shop offers an assortment of old world treasures, crafts and dried flower arrangements. Wedding packages, that can include a minister, are available.

INNKEEPERS:	Barbara Fisher
ADDRESS:	245 Cyteworth; PO Box 540
	Estes Park, CO 80517
TELEPHONE:	(970) 586-5871; (800) 597-7903
E-MAIL:	barbarasbnb@aol.com
WEBSITE:	www.barbarasbnb.com
ROOMS:	3 Rooms; Private & shared baths
CHILDREN:	Welcome
ANIMALS:	Not allowed
HANDICAPPED:	Not handicapped accessible
DIETARY NEEDS:	Will accommodate guests' special dietary needs

Cinnamon Rolls

Makes 12 Rolls

2½	cups milk
2	packages active dry yeast
⅓	cup sugar
⅓	cup oil
2	teaspoons salt
3	teaspoons baking powder
1	egg
6-7	cups flour
½	cup (1 stick) butter, melted

Filling mixture:

¼	cup sugar
1	teaspoon cinnamon
½	cup packed brown sugar

Bring the milk just to below the boiling point; cool to lukewarm. Dissolve the 2 packages of yeast in ½ cup of the lukewarm milk. Add the yeast mixture, sugar, oil, salt, baking powder and egg to the remaining 2 cups of milk. Mix well; then add flour until easy to handle. Knead until smooth. Place dough in a lightly oiled bowl. Cover and allow to rise until doubled in size. Punch down dough and roll into an 18x24-inch rectangle. Cover with the melted butter.

Preheat the oven to 350°F. Combine the filling ingredients and sprinkle on top of the butter. Roll the dough up tightly, jelly-roll fashion, starting with the 24-inch side; seal edges. Cut into 12 (2-inch) slices. At this point, the slices can be frozen, then removed as needed, or placed in a greased pan, refrigerated and covered for up to 48 hours. If refrigerated, take rolls out and allow to rise, if needed.

Bake about 20 minutes, until light brown. Let cool for about 10 minutes and then frost or drizzle with a vanilla glaze, using your favorite recipe.

Bears Inn

In the early 1900's, nearly 50 resorts populated the Evergreen area. Today, the Bears Inn, historically known as Marshdale Lodge, is the single remaining resort. The exposed log beams, hardwood floors and antiques accentuate the charm of that engaging bygone era. A hearty breakfast is served each morning in the captivating great room.

Area activities include biking, fishing, hiking, ice skating, snowshoeing, cross country skiing and golf.

INNKEEPERS:	Darrell & Chris Jenkins
ADDRESS:	27425 Spruce Lane
	Evergreen, CO 80439
TELEPHONE:	(303) 670-1205; (800) 863-1205
E-MAIL:	innkeepers@bearsinn.com
WEBSITE:	www.bearsinn.com
ROOMS:	10 Rooms; 1 Suite; All with private baths
CHILDREN:	Children age 12 and older are welcome
ANIMALS:	Not allowed; Resident dog
HANDICAPPED:	Not handicapped accessible
DIETARY NEEDS:	Will accommodate guests' special dietary needs

Sticky Buns

Makes 24 Rolls

"Sticky" aptly describes these "finger-lickin'-good" caramel-nut rolls. Preparation is a breeze using ready-made, frozen bread dough. Start the night before serving, and just pop them into the oven in the morning. Easy and delicious!

¾   cup chopped pecans
2   (1-pound) packages frozen dough white dinner rolls (12-count)
1   (3-ounce) box vanilla cook-and-serve pudding mix (not instant)
¾   cup (1½ sticks) butter
¾   cup packed brown sugar

Generously grease a 15x10-inch baking pan. Sprinkle the nuts onto the bottom of the pan. Place the frozen rolls evenly over the nuts (there will be space between the rolls). Sprinkle the dry pudding mix over the rolls.

In a medium saucepan, bring the butter and brown sugar to a rolling boil. Pour the hot mixture over the rolls. Coat plastic wrap with nonstick cooking spray and cover the pan. Let the pan stand overnight on the countertop, allowing the rolls to rise.

In the morning, preheat oven to 350°F. Carefully remove the plastic wrap and bake rolls for approximately 25 minutes, or until golden brown. Remove pan from oven and let stand for 2 minutes. Place a cookie sheet over the baking pan and invert to remove rolls. Serve hot from the oven.

Posada de Sol y Sombra

The Posada de Sol y Sombra (Inn of Sun and Shadow) is sequestered behind a white picket fence on a quiet street in the southern Colorado town of La Veta. This 1890's brick farmhouse is situated at the base of Cuchara Valley between the Sangre de Cristo mountain range and the skyscraping Spanish Peaks.

Paintings by local artists enhance the walls of this hospitable inn.

INNKEEPERS:	Betty & Carroll Elwell
ADDRESS:	PO Box 522
	La Veta, CO 81055
TELEPHONE:	(719) 742-3159
E-MAIL:	Not available
WEBSITE:	Not available
ROOMS:	2 Rooms; Shared bath
CHILDREN:	Welcome
ANIMALS:	Not allowed
HANDICAPPED:	Not handicapped accessible
DIETARY NEEDS:	Will accommodate guests' special dietary needs

Dried Cherry Buttermilk Scones

Makes 8 Scones

"These scones have been so well-received, they have become a notable part of our menus. Coming from Michigan, we like to use Michigan products such as Traverse City dried sour cherries." — Betty Elwell, Posada de Sol y Sombra

2	cups all-purpose flour
⅓	cup sugar
1½	teaspoons baking powder
½	teaspoon baking soda
6	tablespoons (¾ stick) butter, chilled
½	cup buttermilk
1	large egg
1½	teaspoons vanilla extract
⅔	cup dried sour cherries

Preheat oven to 400°F. In a large bowl, sift together the flour, sugar, baking powder and baking soda. Cut butter into ½-inch cubes and distribute over flour mixture. With a pastry blender, cut in the butter until the mixture resembles coarse crumbs. In a small bowl, stir together the buttermilk, egg and vanilla; add to the flour mixture and stir just until moistened. Stir in the cherries.

With lightly floured hands, pat the dough into an 8-inch diameter circle on an ungreased cookie sheet. With a serrated knife, cut into 8 wedges. Bake 18-20 minutes, or until a toothpick inserted in the center comes out clean. Cool for 5 minutes. Serve warm.

> *Carol's Corner*
> *The tartness of the cherries complements the sweetness of the biscuit. If you have never tried scones, you must try these!*

Castle Marne

Built in 1889, Castle Marne is considered by many to be the finest example of America's most eclectic architect, William Lang (designer of Unsinkable Molly Brown's house). Its history glows through the hand-rubbed woods, the renowned circular stained glass Peacock Window and the original, ornate fireplace.

"No one can truly own any part of the heritage of a city and its people. That's why we consider ourselves as merely caretakers of the Castle Marne, and it's a privilege we cherish." — Owners, Castle Marne

INNKEEPERS:	Jim & Diane Peiker; Melissa Feher-Peiker
ADDRESS:	1572 Race Street
	Denver, CO 80206
TELEPHONE:	(303) 331-0621; (800) 92-MARNE
E-MAIL:	info@castlemarne.com
WEBSITE:	www.castlemarne.com
ROOMS:	8 Rooms; 1 Suite; All with private baths
CHILDREN:	Children age 10 and older are welcome
ANIMALS:	Not allowed
HANDICAPPED:	Not handicapped accessible
DIETARY NEEDS:	Will accommodate guests' special dietary needs

The Queen's Royal Scones

Makes 12 Scones

"We have tasted scones from many tearooms and truly believe this is the finest recipe we have tasted or made for our teas and Victorian luncheons." — Diane Peiker, Castle Marne

¾   cup currants soaked in liqueur of choice (we use sherry)
3¼   cups all-purpose flour
¾   cup sugar
2½   teaspoons baking powder
½   teaspoon baking soda
¾   cup (1½ sticks) cold butter, cut into small pieces
1   cup buttermilk

Soak currants in liqueur for at least 2 hours. In a large bowl, stir together the flour, sugar, baking powder and baking soda until thoroughly blended. Using a pastry cutter, cut the butter into the flour mixture until it resembles cornmeal. Stir in the drained currants. Make a well in the center of the flour mixture and add the buttermilk all at once. Stir with a fork until the batter pulls away from the side of the bowl.

Preheat oven to 425°F. Gather the dough together into a ball. Put on a lightly floured surface and pat into a circle about ¾-inch high (handle the dough as little as possible). Using a small heart- or daisy-shaped cookie cutter, cut dough into individual scones. Place 1½-inches apart on a lightly greased cookie sheet. Bake for 12 minutes, or until tops are lightly browned. Serve warm with crème fraîche and raspberry jam or honey butter.

Eastholme in the Rockies

Designated a Ute Pass landmark by the 1976 Bicentennial Committee, Eastholme is the oldest of a group of resort hotels that once flourished between the historic towns of Manitou Springs and Cripple Creek. Authentically restored and furnished with antiques, Eastholme was the sole recipient of Colorado's Historical Preservation Award for 1989.

Notable guests have included Dwight and Mamie Eisenhower, a European monarch and, most recently, a lady "ghost."

INNKEEPERS:	Terry Thompson & Family
ADDRESS:	4445 Hagerman; PO Box 98, Cascade, CO 80809
TELEPHONE:	(719) 684-9901
E-MAIL:	info@eastholme.com
WEBSITE:	www.eastholme.com
ROOMS:	4 Rooms; 2 Suites; 2 Cottages; Private & shared baths
CHILDREN:	Welcome
ANIMALS:	Not allowed
HANDICAPPED:	Not handicapped accessible
DIETARY NEEDS:	Will accommodate guests' special dietary needs

Scones

Makes 15 Scones

2½   cups flour
1   tablespoon baking powder
½   cup sugar
½   cup (1 stick) butter, cut into pieces
Buttermilk, as needed

Mix the flour, baking powder and sugar in a food processor with the steel blade. Add the butter a little at a time, until you have the consistency of cornmeal. (At this point, you can put it in a zip lock bag in the refrigerator and keep it for at least a month.)

Preheat oven to 350°F. Take as much of the mixture as you think you will need and add buttermilk slowly, a little at a time until you get a ball of dough, not too soft. If you get it too soft, just add more of the flour mixture. On a lightly floured board, knead the dough slightly and pat flat until it is about ½-inch thick. Cut with a sharp biscuit cutter and place on an ungreased cookie sheet. Bake for 12-15 minutes, or until light golden brown. Serve with jam.

> *Carol's Corner*
> *Using a food processor is a fast and easy way to prepare this "do-ahead" scone mix. You can have warm, tasty scones on the breakfast table in no time at all.*

Pancakes, Waffles & Crêpes

Room at the Inn

I deally situated in the historic center of Colorado Springs, the Room at the Inn retains the charm, romance and gracious hospitality of the Victorian Era. Delightful and romantic, the inn features original hand-painted murals, four Italian-tiled fireplaces, fish scale siding, a wraparound veranda and a three-story turret that overlooks a tree-lined avenue.

Every afternoon, guests are invited to share tea, home-baked goodies and conversation in the main parlor.

INNKEEPERS:	Dorian & Linda Ciolek
ADDRESS:	618 North Nevada Avenue
	Colorado Springs, CO 80903
TELEPHONE:	(719) 442-1896; (888) 442-1896
E-MAIL:	roomatinn@pcisys.net
WEBSITE:	www.roomattheinn.com
ROOMS:	8 Rooms; All with private baths
CHILDREN:	Children age 12 and older are welcome
ANIMALS:	Not allowed
HANDICAPPED:	Is handicapped accessible
DIETARY NEEDS:	Will accommodate guests' special dietary needs

Gingerbread Pancakes with Lemon Sauce

Makes 8 to 10 (4-inch) Pancakes

1⅓	cups all-purpose flour
1	teaspoon baking powder
¼	teaspoon baking soda
¼	teaspoon salt
½	teaspoon ground ginger
1	teaspoon cinnamon
1	egg
1¼	cups milk
¼	cup molasses
3	tablespoons vegetable oil

Lemon sauce (recipe below)

In a large bowl, sift together the flour, baking powder, baking soda, salt, ginger and cinnamon. Make a well in the center of the dry ingredients. In a medium bowl, beat together the egg, milk, molasses and oil. Add the wet ingredients to the dry ingredients and stir until just combined. Preheat a greased griddle or heavy skillet. Pour ¼ cup of batter at a time onto the hot griddle and cook until done. Serve with hot lemon sauce.

Lemon sauce:

½	cup sugar
1	tablespoon cornstarch

Pinch of nutmeg

1	cup cold water
2	tablespoons butter
½	teaspoon grated lemon zest
2	tablespoons fresh lemon juice

In a medium saucepan, combine the sugar, cornstarch and nutmeg. Gradually stir in the water. Cook, stirring over medium heat, until mixture is thick and clear. Add the butter, lemon zest and lemon juice. Stir until butter has melted and mixture is smooth. Serve hot. Makes 1½ cups.

Taharaa Mountain Lodge

S ince its opening in 1997, the Taharaa Mountain Lodge has hosted the management of major corporations as well as family reunions. The lodge offers catered luncheons, dinners and cocktail receptions for groups of up to 30, and meeting and conference facilities for 15.

"I enjoyed your accommodations so much. I appreciated your courtesy and at home hospitality. I look forward to another opportunity to visit Estes Park to see you again." — President & CEO, Honda Motor Company

INNKEEPERS:	Ken & Diane Harlan
ADDRESS:	3110 South Saint Vrain
	Estes Park, CO 80517
TELEPHONE:	(970) 577-0098; (800) 597-0098
E-MAIL:	info@taharaa.com
WEBSITE:	www.taharaa.com
ROOMS:	9 Rooms; 3 Suites; All with private baths
CHILDREN:	Children age 13 and older are welcome
ANIMALS:	Not allowed; Resident dog
HANDICAPPED:	Is handicapped accessible
DIETARY NEEDS:	Will accommodate guests' special dietary needs

Sweet Potato Pancakes

Makes 6 Servings

The pancake batter can be made in advance and refrigerated overnight.

¾   **pound fresh sweet potatoes (or 12-ounces canned)**
1½   **cups all-purpose flour**
3½   **teaspoons baking powder**
1   **teaspoon salt**
½   **teaspoon nutmeg**
½   **teaspoon cinnamon**
2   **eggs, beaten**
1½   **cups milk**
¼   **cup (½ stick) unsalted butter, melted**
Sautéed sliced pears or apples for topping
Powdered sugar for dusting
Fresh fruit for garnish
Syrup for serving

Bring water to a boil in a saucepan. Cook sweet potatoes for about 15 minutes, or until tender, yet still firm (cooking time depends on size). Drain and immediately place in cold water to loosen skins. Drain. Remove skins and mash. (If using canned sweet potatoes, drain, discard liquid and mash.)

In a large bowl, sift together flour, baking powder, salt, nutmeg and cinnamon. In a separate bowl, beat together eggs, milk and melted butter. Add mashed potatoes. Mix well. Add the sweet potato mixture to dry ingredients; stir to form a medium-thick batter with bits of potato still visible.

Preheat a greased griddle or skillet. Spoon batter onto griddle. *Cook about 2 minutes, until undersides are browned. Flip pancakes and cook until done.

Serve 2-3 pancakes per person. Top pancakes with sautéed pears or apples. Garnish plate with colorful fresh fruit. Dust pancakes and fruit topping with powdered sugar. Serve with warm syrup.

*Tip: To make crispy edges, combine half vegetable oil/half melted butter in a squirt bottle. Squeeze a ring of this mixture around edge of each pancake.

Black Dog Inn

Built in 1910, the Black Dog Inn was one of the earliest homes built in Estes Park. Snuggled among towering pine and aspen trees on a rolling acre, it affords an expansive view of Lumpy Ridge and the Estes Valley. A footpath that runs in front of the inn leads to nearby attractions.

The innkeepers, having experience in hiking, skiing and snowshoeing, happily share books, maps and backcountry knowledge with their guests.

INNKEEPERS:	Dee & Norm Pritchard
ADDRESS:	650 South Saint Vrain Avenue; PO Box 4659
	Estes Park, CO 80517
TELEPHONE:	(970) 586-0374
E-MAIL:	dee@blackdoginn.com
WEBSITE:	www.blackdoginn.com
ROOMS:	4 Rooms; All with private baths
CHILDREN:	Children age 12 and older are welcome
ANIMALS:	Not allowed; Resident dog
HANDICAPPED:	Not handicapped accessible
DIETARY NEEDS:	Will accommodate guests' special dietary needs

Whole Wheat Banana Walnut Pancakes

Makes 2 Servings

You'll never want just plain pancakes again! Add a bright red strawberry to the plate for color.

½	cup whole wheat flour
½	cup all-purpose flour
2	teaspoons brown sugar
1	teaspoon baking powder
1	egg
1	cup buttermilk
1	tablespoon vegetable oil
½	teaspoon vanilla extract
2	bananas, sliced
⅓	cup (more or less) chopped walnuts

Whipped cream for serving
Maple syrup for serving

In a large bowl, combine the two flours, brown sugar and baking powder; make a well in the center and set aside. In a small bowl, slightly beat the egg and combine with the buttermilk, oil, and vanilla. Add the wet ingredients to the dry ingredients and stir until smooth. (The batter can be covered and refrigerated overnight, if desired.)

Preheat a lightly greased griddle or skillet. Drop batter from a large spoon to make 4 large (6-inch) pancakes. Top batter with banana slices (reserve some for garnishing the pancakes when serving) and sprinkle with chopped walnuts. When undersides are nicely browned, flip the pancakes over and cook until golden brown. Serve the pancakes topped with chopped or sliced bananas, whipped cream and warm maple syrup.

Steamboat Valley Guest House

Guests of the Steamboat Valley Bed and Breakfast enjoy homemade breakfasts that may include Swedish pancakes, green chili cheese soufflé or a steaming bowl of Irish oatmeal, before a day on the slopes or a hike in the Rockies. Later, they can relax by the wildflower garden.

Business travelers are welcome. As one guest said, "Thanks for making my business trip not feel like business."

INNKEEPERS:	Alice & George Lund
ADDRESS:	1245 Crawford Avenue; PO Box 773815
	Steamboat Springs, CO 80477
TELEPHONE:	(970) 870-9017; (800) 530-3866
E-MAIL:	george@steamboatvalley.com
WEBSITE:	www.steamboatvalley.com
ROOMS:	3 Rooms; 1 Suite; All with private baths
CHILDREN:	Not allowed
ANIMALS:	Not allowed
HANDICAPPED:	Not handicapped accessible
DIETARY NEEDS:	Call ahead for guests with special dietary needs

Swedish Pancakes

Makes 6 to 8 Servings

6	eggs
¼	cup sugar
½	cup (1 stick) butter, melted
¾	teaspoon salt
2¼	cups flour
5	cups milk
½	cup lingonberries
Sour cream	

Separate eggs. Place whites in a small bowl, cover and refrigerate. Place egg yolks in large mixing bowl and beat with sugar until a pale yellow. Blend in butter and salt. Gradually add flour alternately with milk and beat until smooth. Cover and refrigerate a few hours or overnight.

To cook, oil hot griddle lightly. Beat egg whites to soft peaks and carefully fold into batter. Use dipper to make small cakes and brown lightly on both sides. Serve immediately in small stacks on heated plates. Top each serving with 1 tablespoon lingonberries and a dollop of sour cream.

> *Carol's Corner*
> *These pancakes are very thin and delicate, almost like crêpes. Doreen's husband, Don, is of Swedish descent and is very fond of Swedish pancakes. His mother rolls the pancakes with lingonberry sauce inside. The above recipe will work for rolled pancakes. Fill with any fruit filling of your choice.*

Cattail Creek Inn

Staying in bed and breakfast inns in the United States and around the world, and experiencing that personalized style of travel has been a highlight and a focus for the owners of the Cattail Creek Inn.

Out of their love of these experiences, and the enjoyment of hosting travelers in their home, the Buchmans have incorporated the amenities and features of the finest bed and breakfasts inns into their Cattail Creek Inn.

INNKEEPERS:	Sue & Harold Buchman
ADDRESS:	2665 Abarr Drive
	Loveland, CO 80538
TELEPHONE:	(970) 667-7600; (800) 572-2466
E-MAIL:	info@cattailcreekinn.com
WEBSITE:	www.cattailcreekinn.com
ROOMS:	8 Rooms; All with private baths
CHILDREN:	Children age 14 and older are welcome
ANIMALS:	Not allowed
HANDICAPPED:	Is handicapped accessible
DIETARY NEEDS:	Will accommodate guests' special dietary needs

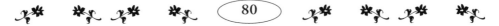

Pecan Belgian Waffles with Sautéed Peaches

Makes 2 Servings

1   cup all-purpose flour
2   teaspoons baking powder
⅛   teaspoon salt
1   cup milk
2   eggs, separated
½   cup (1 stick) butter, melted and cooled
½   cup finely chopped pecans

Sautéed peaches:
1   tablespoon butter
1½ cups fresh peaches, peeled and sliced
¼   cup sugar
2   tablespoons peach brandy
2   fresh strawberries, sliced for garnish
Powdered sugar for garnish

In a large bowl, sift together the flour, baking powder and salt. In a small bowl, combine the milk and egg yolks, separating the egg whites into another bowl. Beat the egg whites until stiff peaks form (this is the key to the recipe – the egg whites must be stiff). Add the egg yolk mixture to the dry ingredients. Stir just until ingredients are moist. Stir in the cooled butter. Gently fold in the stiff egg whites. Fold in the chopped pecans.

Preheat a standard Belgian waffle iron. Pour the batter onto the waffle iron and cook until the waffles are golden brown, making 3 sets of 2 waffles.

To sauté the peaches, melt 1 tablespoon of butter in a medium skillet. Sauté the peaches for a few minutes; add the sugar and brandy. Cook on low heat, stirring occasionally, for 10-15 minutes.

To serve, place the waffles on serving plates; top with the sautéed peaches. Add the sliced strawberries for color; dust with powdered sugar. Beautiful!

Lookout Inn Guest House

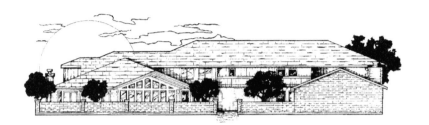

Warmly elegant and quiet, the Lookout Inn Guest House features lodging in the European style while offering all of the amenities of a large hotel. Full-service conference and meeting rooms, ideal for weekend retreats, seminars and all types of meetings, can easily be arranged.

The great room and patio provide a lovely atmosphere for special events such as weddings, rehearsal dinners and corporate cocktail parties. They also host murder mysteries!

INNKEEPERS:	Lonnie Dooley
ADDRESS:	6901 Lookout Road
	Boulder, CO 80301
TELEPHONE:	(303) 530-1513
E-MAIL:	info@guest-house.com
WEBSITE:	www.guest-house.com
ROOMS:	13 Rooms; All with private baths
CHILDREN:	Call ahead
ANIMALS:	Not allowed
HANDICAPPED:	Is handicapped accessible
DIETARY NEEDS:	Will accommodate guests' special dietary needs

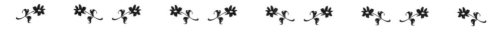

Whole Wheat Buttermilk Waffles

Makes 12 (4-inch) Waffles

"As we are an inn that caters primarily to corporate travelers — we have a lot of repeat guests. One of our regulars once mentioned incorporating something a bit different into our standard Continental-plus breakfast. He suggested waffles. (Most of our guests prefer low-fat, healthy breakfasts, like bagels, cereal, etc.) We decided to start 'Waffle Wednesdays,' and it has become so much fun, and so popular with the guests, that I think some of them even plan their business trips so they can be here for it! We always use this recipe and offer several toppings (blueberries, peaches, bananas, walnuts, etc.) It's been several years of doing this now, and that same guest still stays here. Even when we're full, those that have to stay at a different hotel will come for waffles — and we never charge them!"
— *Lonnie Dooley, Lookout Inn Guest House*

¾   cup whole wheat flour
¾   cup all-purpose flour
2   teaspoons baking powder
¾   teaspoon baking soda
½   teaspoon salt
2   tablespoons sugar
3   eggs
1½   cups buttermilk
¾   cup (1½ sticks) butter, melted
¼   cup milk, if needed

Put the flours into a small mixing bowl. Add the baking powder, baking soda, salt and sugar. Stir with a fork to blend. In a large mixing bowl, beat eggs and combine with buttermilk and butter. Add dry ingredients to wet ingredients and stir just until combined. If batter is too thick, add a small amount of milk. Cook on hot waffle iron until done.

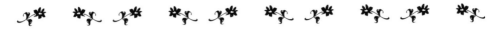

Room at the Inn

B uilt in 1896, the Room at the Inn is a classic Queen Anne Victorian that has been carefully restored to its original elegance with the added luxury and comfort of modern amenities.

A full breakfast, served on fine china, includes homemade muffins and breakfast breads, seasonal fresh fruit and a hot entrée. Favorites include gingerbread pancakes with lemon sauce, buttermilk buckwheat waffles with raspberry sauce and baked Denver omelettes.

INNKEEPERS:	Dorian & Linda Ciolek
ADDRESS:	618 North Nevada Avenue
	Colorado Springs, CO 80903
TELEPHONE:	(719) 442-1896; (888) 442-1896
E-MAIL:	roomatinn@pcisys.net
WEBSITE:	www.roomattheinn.com
ROOMS:	8 Rooms; All with private baths
CHILDREN:	Children age 12 and older are welcome
ANIMALS:	Not accepted
HANDICAPPED:	Is handicapped accessible
DIETARY NEEDS:	Will accommodate guests' special dietary needs

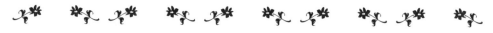

Buckwheat Buttermilk Waffles

Makes 4 to 6 (7-inch) Waffles

1	cup unbleached white flour
¼	cup buckwheat flour
¼	cup whole wheat flour
2	teaspoons baking powder
¾	teaspoon baking soda
½	teaspoon salt
2	tablespoons sugar
3	eggs
1½	cups buttermilk
½	cup (1 stick) butter, melted and cooled

Fresh raspberries for garnish
Whipped cream for garnish
Butter for serving
Raspberry syrup for serving

Preheat waffle iron. In a large bowl, sift together the flours, baking powder, baking soda, salt and sugar. In a medium bowl, beat together the eggs, buttermilk and melted butter. Add the egg mixture to the dry ingredients; mix just until blended. Cook the batter on the hot waffle iron until waffles are golden brown. Garnish each serving plate with fresh raspberries and whipped cream. Serve with butter and raspberry syrup.

Engelmann Pines

From its Rocky Mountain perch, this spacious, modern lodge offers spectacular views of the Continental Divide. A free bus shuttles skiers from the front door to some of Colorado's best ski slopes. Cross-country ski aficionados will find trails just across the road.

When the snow melts, guests enjoy golfing, hiking, biking, fishing and horseback riding. In the mornings, eager sports enthusiasts fill up on marzipan cake, muesli and fresh fruit crêpes.

INNKEEPERS:	Heinz & Margaret Engel
ADDRESS:	PO Box 1305
	Winter Park, CO 80482
TELEPHONE:	(970) 726-4632; (800) 992-9512
E-MAIL:	margaretengelwp@aol.com
WEBSITE:	www.engelmannpines.com
ROOMS:	7 Rooms; Private and shared baths
CHILDREN:	Welcome
ANIMALS:	Not allowed
HANDICAPPED:	Not handicapped accessible
DIETARY NEEDS:	Will accommodate guests' special dietary needs

Crab Crêpes

Makes 8 Servings

Crab mixture:
2	tablespoons butter
2	tablespoons flour
1	cup milk
1	(8-ounce) package cream cheese
1	pound crab meat, or imitation crab
2	tablespoons ketchup

Szechuan seasoning, to taste

Melt butter in a heavy pan. Add flour and stir with a wire whisk, being careful not to burn the mixture. Add milk and continue whisking until it begins to thicken. Add cream cheese and stir until melted. Add crab meat, ketchup and Szechuan seasoning. Set aside and make the crêpes.

Crêpe batter:
4	eggs
½	cup milk
½	cup water
2	tablespoons butter, melted
1	teaspoon vanilla extract
2	teaspoons sugar
½	teaspoon salt
1	cup flour

Mix together all ingredients, except flour, with electric mixer until well blended. Add flour and continue to mix until all lumps are gone. Heat a 5-inch nonstick skillet over medium heat. The batter will grease the pan, but you may need a few drops of oil to start. Add a small amount of batter and rotate the pan to spread the batter evenly. Brown gently on both sides. When the crêpes are done, fill them with the warm crab mixture and serve.

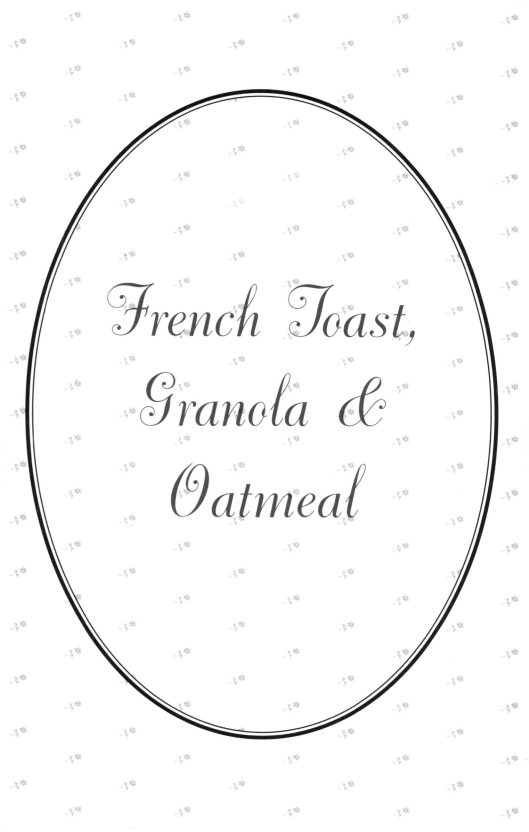

French Toast, Granola & Oatmeal

Fireside Inn

An American Youth Hostel during the summer, the Fireside Inn is a converted 1880's Victorian house in Breckenridge's historic district. Accommodations for this unique bed and breakfast include a suite, rooms with private baths and dorm facilities with shared baths.

A sign in the breakfast room says, "Life's too short not to live in Colorado."

INNKEEPERS:	Niki & Andy Harris
ADDRESS:	114 North French Street; PO Box 2252
	Breckenridge, CO 80424
TELEPHONE:	(970) 453-6456
E-MAIL:	info@firesideinn.com
WEBSITE:	www.firesideinn.com
ROOMS:	3 Rooms; 1 Suite; All with private baths
	5 Dorm rooms; All with shared baths
CHILDREN:	Children under age 12 are free in private rooms
ANIMALS:	Not allowed
HANDICAPPED:	Not handicapped accessible
DIETARY NEEDS:	Will accommodate guests' special dietary needs

Sourdough Cinnamon French Toast

Makes 2 to 3 Servings

3	eggs
⅛	teaspoon nutmeg
1	teaspoon cinnamon
¼	cup milk

Dash of sugar
6 slices sourdough French bread
Fireside Inn maple syrup (recipe below)

Beat together eggs, nutmeg, cinnamon, milk and sugar. Dip bread in egg mixture and cook on a preheated, greased griddle or skillet. Serve with Fireside Inn maple syrup.

Fireside Inn maple syrup:
2½ cups water
2¼ cups packed light brown sugar
1¼ cups white sugar
1 tablespoon maple extract
Dash of vanilla extract

Mix all ingredients in a saucepan. Bring to a boil, stirring occasionally. Simmer for 30 minutes. Cool. Store leftover syrup in refrigerator. Makes 1 quart.

Shenandoah Inn

The Shenandoah Inn Bed and Breakfast is a recently restored home on two private riverfront acres on the Gold Medal trout waters of the Frying Pan River. Within walking distance of the restaurants and shops of Basalt, it is centrally located 20 minutes from Aspen and 25 minutes from the Glenwood hot springs pool.

With 20 years of professional cooking experience, Bob Ziets, the owner, treats guests to a full gourmet breakfast.

INNKEEPERS:	Bob & Terri Ziets
ADDRESS:	0600 Frying Pan Road; PO Box 578
	Basalt, CO 81621
TELEPHONE:	(970) 927-4991; (800) 804-5520
E-MAIL:	www.shenandoahinn.com/mailbox.html
WEBSITE:	www.shenandoahinn.com
ROOMS:	4 Rooms; Private baths; 1 Cabin that sleeps 4
CHILDREN:	Well-behaved children age 12 and older are welcome
ANIMALS:	Not allowed
HANDICAPPED:	Not handicapped accessible
DIETARY NEEDS:	Will accommodate guests' special dietary needs

Orange Crumb French Toast

Makes 3 to 4 Servings

2	eggs
¼	teaspoon salt
⅔	cup fresh squeezed orange juice
2	tablespoons Grand Marnier (optional)
¾	cup corn flake crumbs
3	teaspoons grated orange zest (reserve 1 teaspoon for garnish)
8	(¾-inch thick) slices day-old French bread
3	tablespoons sweet butter

Orange syrup (recipe below)

In a medium bowl, whisk together eggs, salt, orange juice and Grand Marnier. On a plate, combine cereal crumbs with 2 teaspoons of the grated orange zest. Dip bread into egg mixture, then dip into cereal crumbs. Coat evenly on all sides.

Melt butter in skillet. Brown both sides of bread. Drain on paper towels. Arrange French toast on warm plates and lightly dust with remaining grated orange zest. Serve with warm orange syrup.

Orange syrup:

1	cup Vermont maple syrup
¼	cup fresh squeezed orange juice
1	teaspoon grated orange zest
¼	cup (½ stick) butter

Combine syrup ingredients in saucepan. Simmer 5 minutes.

✻ Carol's Corner

The syrup can be made ahead and refrigerated. It can even be frozen. Warm in microwave before serving. Delicious!

St. Elmo Hotel

Guests step back in time and relive the glory days of Colorado's colorful past at the St. Elmo Hotel in Ouray. Once bustling with gold and silver seekers, Ouray is today a picturesque hamlet, nestled in the soaring and spectacular San Juan mountains of southwestern Colorado.

Furnished with antiques, stained glass, polished wood and brass trim throughout, the St. Elmo Hotel offers a charming lobby, cozy parlor and sunny breakfast room.

INNKEEPERS:	**Dan & Sandy Lingenfelter**
ADDRESS:	**426 Main Street; PO Box 667**
	Ouray, CO 81427
TELEPHONE:	**(970) 325-4951**
E-MAIL:	innkeeper@stelmohotel.com
WEBSITE:	www.stelmohotel.com
ROOMS:	9 Rooms; All with private baths
CHILDREN:	Welcome
ANIMALS:	Not allowed
HANDICAPPED:	Not handicapped accessible
DIETARY NEEDS:	Will accommodate guests' special dietary needs

Orange French Toast

Makes 6 Servings

6   **eggs**
1   **cup orange juice**
⅓   **cup milk**
¼   **teaspoon vanilla extract**
¼   **teaspoon salt**
Finely grated zest of 1 orange
12   **(¾-inch thick) slices French bread**
Maple syrup for serving

Beat eggs in a large bowl. Add orange juice, milk, vanilla, salt and orange zest. Mix well.

Dip bread in egg mixture, turning to coat all sides. Place on a baking sheet in a single layer. Pour any remaining egg mixture over the top and turn slices over a couple of times. Cover with plastic wrap and put in refrigerator overnight.

Preheat a greased griddle or skillet. Cook the slices until golden brown on both sides. Serve with maple syrup.

Main Street B&B

Surrounded by the San Juan mountains, the Main Street Bed and Breakfast is located in historic Ouray, where virtually all the buildings built between 1880 and 1900 have been preserved. Nestled in a canyon, the entire town is listed on the National Registry of Historic Places.

In 1896, the discovery of high-grade gold ore by Thomas Walsh prompted the establishment of the Camp Bird Mine. The total value of ores mined exceeded 27 million dollars by 1916.

INNKEEPERS:	Paul & Becky-Klein McCreary
ADDRESS:	334 Main Street
	Ouray, CO 81427
TELEPHONE:	(970) 325-4871; (970) 325-4317
E-MAIL:	mainstreet@gwe.net
WEBSITE:	www.colorado-bnb.com/mainst
ROOMS:	3 Rooms; 1 Cottage; All with private baths
CHILDREN:	Welcome in the cottage
ANIMALS:	Not allowed
HANDICAPPED:	Not handicapped accessible
DIETARY NEEDS:	Will accommodate guests' special dietary needs

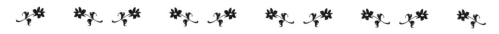

Baked Peach French Toast

Makes 6 Servings

A breakfast treat the whole family will love.

1	(3-ounce) package cream cheese, room temperature
10	(1-inch thick) slices French bread
1	(29-ounce) can peach slices in light or heavy syrup, drained
¼	cup chopped nuts (optional)
10	maraschino cherries, with or without stems
3	eggs
1	cup milk
⅓	cup maple-flavored syrup
2	tablespoons butter, melted
1	tablespoon sugar
1	teaspoon cinnamon
1	teaspoon vanilla extract

Preheat oven to 350°F. Coat a 13x9-inch baking dish with nonstick cooking spray. Lightly spread cream cheese on both sides of the bread. Place the bread into the prepared dish and prick each piece several times with a fork. Place peach slices over top of bread. Sprinkle nuts (if using) over peaches. Top each slice with a cherry.

In a large bowl, whisk together the eggs, milk, syrup, melted butter, sugar, cinnamon and vanilla. Pour mixture over the bread. Bake for 20-30 minutes, or until French toast is set in the middle.

Crystal Dreams

Located between majestic red cliffs and a meandering river, the Crystal Dreams Bed and Breakfast and Spa is truly a magical place. While staying at this romantic Victorian-style house, guests might spy Bighorn sheep or deer traversing the edges of the magnificent Rocky Mountains or Canadian geese playing at the edge of the enchanting Crystal River.

Luxurious skin and facial care, including European facials and therapeutic massages, are available upon request.

INNKEEPERS:	Lisa & Steve Wagner
ADDRESS:	0475 Redstone Boulevard
	Redstone, CO 81623
TELEPHONE:	(970) 963-8240
E-MAIL:	redstone@rof.net
WEBSITE:	www.redstonecolorado.com/crystaldreams
ROOMS:	3 Rooms; All with private baths
CHILDREN:	Children age 12 and older are welcome
ANIMALS:	Not allowed
HANDICAPPED:	Not handicapped accessible
DIETARY NEEDS:	Will accommodate guests' special dietary needs

Lisa's Hawaiian French Toast

Makes 4 Servings

Instead of the usual French bread, this French toast calls for Hawaiian sweet bread — a bread with a unique taste and cake-like texture. It is available in the bread aisle or deli section of most grocery stores.

1   **(16-ounce) round loaf King's Hawaiian sweet bread**
Guava jam (or any other jam of choice)
2   **eggs**
1   **cup milk**
Dash of nutmeg
Berries for topping
Powdered sugar for garnish

Slice the bread into 4 very thick slices. Then cut each slice in half to make 8 halves. Make a slit in the middle of the straight edge of each half to form a "pocket." Spoon a couple teaspoons of jam into each pocket.

In a medium bowl, beat together the eggs, milk and nutmeg. Dip each stuffed bread slice into the egg mixture (do not soak).

Heat a greased skillet or griddle. Cook the slices until golden brown on both sides. Place 2 slices of the French toast on each of 4 plates. Top with berries and garnish with a sprinkling of powdered sugar.

The Manor

The Manor was built in 1890 during Ouray's mining boom. This meticulously restored Georgian Victorian hybrid, listed on the National Historic Register, is the recipient of The Historical Society's Preservation Award for "noteworthy restoration of a historical building."

Known as the Switzerland of America, the high peaks and wilderness that surround The Manor create a majestic setting.

INNKEEPERS:	John & Kay Gowins
ADDRESS:	317 Second Street; PO Box 1165
	Ouray, CO 81427
TELEPHONE:	(970) 325-4574
E-MAIL:	themanor@ouraycolorado.net
WEBSITE:	www.ouraycolorado.com
ROOMS:	7 Rooms; All with private baths
CHILDREN:	Can accommodate one child age 5 or older
ANIMALS:	Not allowed
HANDICAPPED:	Not handicapped accessible
DIETARY NEEDS:	Will accommodate guests' special dietary needs

Upside-Down Apple French Toast

Makes 6 Servings

Prepare the night before, or at least 3 hours in advance.

½   cup (1 stick) butter
1¼   cups packed brown sugar
1   tablespoon water
3   Granny Smith apples, peeled, cored and sliced
Cinnamon to taste
½   cup raisins, optional
1   loaf French bread, sliced 1½-inches thick
1½   cups milk
6   eggs
1   teaspoon vanilla
Nutmeg to taste
½   cup whipping cream
½   cup sour cream
¼   cup sugar
½   teaspoon almond extract
Sliced almonds for garnish

Coat a 13x9-inch baking dish with nonstick cooking spray. Combine butter, brown sugar and water in a saucepan over medium heat. Cook, stirring, until just bubbling. Pour into baking dish. Allow to cool for 20-30 minutes. Place apple slices in rows, close together (or overlapping), on top of the mixture in pan. Sprinkle with cinnamon and raisins. Place bread on top of the apples. Mix milk, eggs and vanilla. Pour over bread. Sprinkle with nutmeg. Cover and refrigerate for 3 hours, or overnight.

Preheat oven to 350°F. Bake French toast for 60 minutes, or until golden brown and crispy. Just before the French toast is done baking, whip the whipping cream, sour cream, white sugar and almond extract together on high until thickened. Serve the French toast upside-down. Spoon the sauce in the dish over the French toast. Place 2 tablespoons of whipped cream atop each serving and garnish with almonds.

The Garden House

Located in the heart of Colorado's wine and orchard country, The Garden House Bed and Breakfast has its own small fruit orchard. This spacious tri-level country home features beautiful oak floors, high-beamed ceilings and large bay windows.

Area activities include hiking, biking, wine tasting at six Palisade wineries, snowshoeing, downhill and cross-country skiing and shopping in Grand Junction's charming downtown district.

INNKEEPERS:	Bill & Joyce Haas
ADDRESS:	3587 G Road
	Palisade, CO 81526
TELEPHONE:	(970) 464-4686; (800) 305-4686
E-MAIL:	bjgardenhouse@cs.com
WEBSITE:	www.colorado-bnb.com/gardnhse
ROOMS:	2 Rooms; 2 Suites; All with private baths
CHILDREN:	Children age 12 and older are welcome
ANIMALS:	Not allowed; Resident dog & outside cat
HANDICAPPED:	Not handicapped accessible
DIETARY NEEDS:	Will accommodate guests' special dietary needs

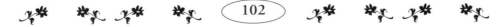

Baked Blueberry Pecan French Toast

Makes 8 Servings

Note: This French toast needs to be refrigerated overnight before baking.

1	(16-ounce) loaf, long and narrow French bread
5	large eggs
1	cup heavy whipping cream
¼	cup orange juice
½	cup plus ⅓ cup brown sugar
2	teaspoons cinnamon
½	teaspoon nutmeg
2	tablespoons butter, melted
1	cup fresh or frozen blueberries
1	cup pecan halves

Blueberry syrup for serving

Coat two 13x9-inch baking dishes generously with nonstick cooking spray. Cut the bread into 16 slices (1-inch thick). Arrange 8 slices in a single layer in each of the two baking dishes. In a large bowl, beat together the eggs, cream, orange juice, ½ cup brown sugar, 1 teaspoon cinnamon and the nutmeg. Dip each slice of bread into the egg mixture, coating both sides, and place it back in the baking dish. If there is any remaining egg mixture, pour it over the bread evenly.

To make the topping, mix ⅓ cup brown sugar and 1 teaspoon cinnamon in a small bowl. Sprinkle the topping over the soaked bread slices. Drizzle with the melted butter. Place the blueberries and pecans on top of the slices; press them into the bread gently, so they don't fall off during baking. Cover the dishes and chill for at least 8 hours.

Preheat oven to 350°F. Bake for approximately 20-25 minutes, or until done. Watch carefully; don't overcook. Serve with warm blueberry syrup.

Maxwell House

Built in 1898, the Maxwell House Bed and Breakfast is a historic landmark house located near downtown Castle Rock. Fully renovated, this delightfully charming bed and breakfast is a step back in time when the spirit of homes was centered around comfort, relaxation and visiting with friends.

The casual country décor features original pinewood floors, handmade quilts, antiques and a piano in the parlor.

INNKEEPERS:	Becky Thomas
ADDRESS:	15 Lewis Street
	Castle Rock, CO 80104
TELEPHONE:	(303) 688-4792
E-MAIL:	info@castlerockbandb.com
WEBSITE:	www.castlerockbandb.com
ROOMS:	2 Rooms; 1 with private bath
CHILDREN:	Call ahead
ANIMALS:	Not allowed
HANDICAPPED:	Not handicapped accessible
DIETARY NEEDS:	Will accommodate guests' special dietary needs

Ann's Sweet Strata

Makes 6 Servings

Start this recipe the night before serving, as the strata needs to soak overnight. The accompanying apricot-orange syrup is delicious and so easy to make!

12	slices firm, white bread (regular-sliced)
3	eggs
2	cups half & half
½	cup plus ⅓ cup sugar
2	teaspoon vanilla extract, divided
12	ounces cream cheese, room temperature
1	egg

Dash of nutmeg
Apricot-orange syrup (recipe below)

Coat a 13x9-inch baking dish with nonstick cooking spray. Trim crusts from bread and arrange 6 slices to cover the bottom of the dish, cutting to fit, if necessary. In a medium bowl, beat eggs, half & half, ½ cup sugar and 1 teaspoon vanilla. Pour half of the egg mixture over the bread in the dish.

To make the filling, beat together the cream cheese, ⅓ cup sugar, egg and 1 teaspoon vanilla in a medium bowl. Drop the filling by small spoonfuls over the moistened bread. Spread gently to cover. Place remaining 6 slices of bread over the filling. Pour remaining egg mixture over the top. Sprinkle with nutmeg. Cover with foil; refrigerate overnight.

Preheat oven to 350°F. Bake, covered, for 30 minutes. Remove foil and bake, uncovered, for an additional 20 minutes, or until puffy. Let stand for 10 minutes before serving. Serve with warm apricot-orange syrup.

Apricot-orange syrup:

1½	cups apricot jam
½	cup orange juice

In a small saucepan, heat together the jam and orange juice. Stir well and serve warm. Note: The syrup can be made ahead and refrigerated. Reheat in the microwave or on the stovetop. Makes 2 cups.

Lavender Swing

B uilt at the turn-of-the-twentieth-century, the Lavender Swing Bed and Breakfast celebrates the charm and elegance of a by-gone era. Positioned at the base of the scenic Rocky Mountains, guests enjoy brilliant blue skies and soothing tangerine and coral sunsets.

Scrumptious breakfasts include fresh baked breads, enticing entrées and specially brewed coffees, served family style in a chandelier-lit dining room.

INNKEEPERS:	Pat Means & Carolyn Goller
ADDRESS:	802 Palmer Avenue
	Glenwood Springs, CO 81601
TELEPHONE:	(970) 945-8289
E-MAIL:	lavender@rof.net
WEBSITE:	www.lavenderswing.com
ROOMS:	3 Rooms; All with private baths
CHILDREN:	Children age 15 and older are welcome
ANIMALS:	Not allowed; Resident parrot "Sally"
HANDICAPPED:	Not handicapped accessible
DIETARY NEEDS:	Will accommodate guests' special dietary needs

Baked Fruit Preserve Croissants

Makes 6 Servings

The day before serving, assemble these individual breakfast entrées and refrigerate them overnight. In the morning, remember to let them stand at room temperature for 45 minutes before baking.

6	croissants, sliced into top and bottom halves
⅔	cup strawberry or peach preserves or orange marmalade
⅓	cup apple juice (or use orange juice with orange marmalade)
6	eggs
1	cup heavy cream
1	teaspoon vanilla extract
6	strawberries or 6 peach slices or 6 half slices of orange for garnish

Whipped cream topping for garnish

Coat 6 individual 5x2½-inch baking dishes with nonstick cooking spray. Place one croissant bottom half in each dish. In a small bowl, thin the preserves or marmalade with the fruit juice. Stir until well mixed. Spoon 2 to 2½ tablespoons of the mixture over each croissant half in the dishes. Cover with the top half on each croissant.

In a large bowl, beat together the eggs, cream and vanilla; pour the mixture evenly over the croissants. (If there is any remaining fruit juice/preserve mixture, it can be spooned over the tops of the croissants, as well.) Cover the dishes; refrigerate overnight.

In the morning, remove the dishes from the refrigerator and let them stand at room temperature for at least 45 minutes. Preheat oven to 350°F. Bake for 30 minutes. Remove the croissants with a spatula and serve on warmed plates. Garnish each serving with fresh fruit and whipped cream.

Inn on Mapleton Hill

Winner of Boulder's Historic Preservation Award in 1992, the Inn on Mapleton Hill boasts individually decorated rooms. Furnishings include marble fireplaces, claw foot tubs, rockers, wicker chairs, Victorian writing desks and antique art.

"During our life, we have traveled to many places, but our brief stay at your inn has been the most enjoyable by far." — Guest, Inn on Mapleton Hill

INNKEEPERS:	Judi & Ray Schultze
ADDRESS:	1001 Spruce Street
	Boulder, CO 80302
TELEPHONE:	(303) 449-6528
E-MAIL:	maphillinn@aol.com
WEBSITE:	www.innonmapletonhill.com
ROOMS:	7 Rooms; 2 Suites; Private & shared baths
CHILDREN:	Children age 12 and older are welcome
ANIMALS:	Not allowed
HANDICAPPED:	Not handicapped accessible
DIETARY NEEDS:	Will accommodate guests' special dietary needs

Judi's Granola

Makes 3½ Cups

"It seems that everyone who comes to the inn loves this granola. I've gotten more requests for it than any other recipe. You'll find it one of the easiest things to make and very healthy, since it's low in fat. Enjoy!" — *Judi Schultze, Inn on Mapleton Hill*

2   cups rolled oats (not instant oats)
2   tablespoons wheat germ
2   tablespoons shredded coconut
¼   cup roasted, unsalted sunflower seeds
2   tablespoons packed brown sugar
2   tablespoons canola oil
¼   cup honey
1   teaspoon vanilla extract
Dash of salt

Preheat oven to 350°F. In a large bowl, combine all of the ingredients; mix thoroughly with a fork. Spread the mixture evenly in a 13x9-inch metal baking pan or on a similarly sized, rimmed baking sheet.

Bake for 12-15 minutes. Remove from oven, stir and re-spread the granola. Bake for about 5 minutes longer (watch carefully so the granola doesn't burn), or until the granola is golden brown and the whole house smells wonderful!

Stir the granola occasionally as it cools (to keep it from sticking to the pan). Let granola cool completely before storing in an airtight container.

Lookout Inn Guest House

The Lookout Inn Guest House offers tastefully decorated suites with fireplaces, kitchenettes and private baths. Some suites include a separate sitting room and private whirlpool bath.

The Guest House is near Boulder County's high tech industries, residential areas and major highways. The full-service conference and meeting rooms are ideal for weekend retreats, seminars and all types of meetings.

INNKEEPERS:	Lonnie Dooley
ADDRESS:	6901 Lookout Road
	Boulder, CO 80301
TELEPHONE:	(303) 530-1513
E-MAIL:	info@guest-house.com
WEBSITE:	www.guest-house.com
ROOMS:	13 Rooms; All with private baths
CHILDREN:	Call ahead
ANIMALS:	Not allowed
HANDICAPPED:	Not handicapped accessible
DIETARY NEEDS:	Will accommodate guests' special dietary needs

Guest House Granola

Makes 4 Quarts

"This granola was brought to the Guest House in 1986 by the very first innkeeper here. It is so popular and the requests for the recipe were so numerous, we finally had it printed. We also have several local residents that buy it to have at home." — Lonnie Dooley, Lookout Inn Guest House

5	cups rolled oats (not instant oats)
1½	cups raw sunflower seeds (salted or unsalted, your preference)
1½	cups wheat germ
1½	cups shredded coconut
1½	cups flaked bran (or All Bran)
1½	cups chopped pecans
1½	cups chopped walnuts
1½	cups slivered almonds
¾	cup raw sesame seeds
¾	cup vegetable or canola oil
¾	cup honey
¾	cup molasses
1½	teaspoons almond extract
1½	teaspoons vanilla extract
2	cups raisins

Combine oats, sunflower seeds, wheat germ, coconut, bran, pecans, walnuts, almonds and sesame seeds in a very large bowl and set aside.

Preheat oven to 350°F. In a saucepan, bring oil, honey, molasses, almond extract and vanilla extract to a boil and cook for 4 minutes, or until thoroughly blended. Pour slowly over the dry ingredients in the bowl and gently stir to mix.

Spread the granola evenly on two baking sheets and bake for 5-8 minutes. Remove from oven and stir all ingredients. Return to the oven for 4 minutes; remove from oven and stir. Repeat 3 or 4 more times. Watch carefully, so it doesn't get too brown. Cool thoroughly and sprinkle with raisins. Note: If granola clumps, return it to the oven and toast a bit more.

Eagle Cliff House

Nancy Conrin, owner of Eagle Cliff House, is a backpacking and hiking consultant who is familiar with regulations and types of equipment. She gladly helps guests plan treks into Rocky Mountain National Park for a day hike or an overnight backcountry experience.

Eagle Cliff House offers individualized services for birthdays, weddings, honeymoons, anniversaries or other special occasions.

INNKEEPERS:	Nancy Conrin
ADDRESS:	2383 Highway 66; PO Box 4312
	Estes Park, CO 80517
TELEPHONE:	(970) 586-5425
E-MAIL:	nancy@eaglecliffhouse.com
WEBSITE:	www.eaglecliffhouse.com
ROOMS:	2 Rooms; 1 Cottage; All with private baths
CHILDREN:	Welcome
ANIMALS:	Not allowed; Outdoor resident pets
HANDICAPPED:	Not handicapped accessible
DIETARY NEEDS:	Will accommodate guests' special dietary needs

Baked Oatmeal

Makes 3 to 4 Servings

A delicious and different way to enjoy an old time breakfast favorite. A warm bowl of this distinctive oatmeal before hiking in the mountains can't be beat.

½	cup chopped walnuts
½	cup packed brown sugar
1	cup rolled oats (not instant oats)
1	apple, peeled and sliced
¼	cup (½ stick) butter, melted
½	teaspoon nutmeg
2	teaspoons cinnamon
¼	teaspoon cloves
2	cups apple juice

Preheat oven to 325°F. Coat a 9x9-inch baking pan with nonstick cooking spray. In a medium bowl, combine walnuts, brown sugar, oats, sliced apple, melted butter, nutmeg, cinnamon and cloves. Mix well. Sprinkle the mixture onto the bottom of the prepared pan. Pour the apple juice over the entire mixture. Do not stir. Bake for 45 minutes, or until bubbly around the edges.

Egg Dishes &
Breakfast Entrées

Logwood

Logwood Bed and Breakfast is located 12 miles north of Durango and 13 miles south of Purgatory Ski Resort, just off the Million Dollar Highway 550, on the banks of the Animas River. All of the guestrooms have large picture windows and are attractively furnished with colorful home-stitched quilts to match the inn's Western decor.

Throughout the day, award-winning homemade desserts, fresh coffee, tea, hot chocolate, cider and soft drinks are available for guests.

INNKEEPERS:	The Windmuellers
ADDRESS:	35060 U.S. Highway 550 North
	Durango, CO 81301
TELEPHONE:	(970) 259-4396; (800) 369-4082
E-MAIL:	paul@durango-logwoodinn.com
WEBSITE:	www.durango-logwoodinn.com
ROOMS:	7 Rooms; 2 Suites; All with private baths
CHILDREN:	Welcome
ANIMALS:	Not allowed; Resident cats
HANDICAPPED:	Not handicapped accessible
DIETARY NEEDS:	Will accommodate guests' special dietary needs

Green Chile & Canadian Bacon Casserole

Makes 8 Servings

Canadian bacon adds a smoky flavor to this casserole.

12   corn tortillas, cut into long, thin strips
16   slices Canadian bacon, each cut into fourths
4   fresh roasted or canned green chiles, peeled, seeded and chopped
1   cup (4 ounces) shredded Monterey Jack cheese
10   eggs
1   cup milk (any kind)
1   cup (4 ounces) shredded cheddar cheese
Salsa for topping
Sour cream for topping

Preheat oven to 350°F Coat a 13x9-inch glass baking dish with nonstick cooking spray.

Place tortilla strips on the bottom of the baking dish to cover evenly. Place half of the cut Canadian bacon pieces over the tortillas. Spread the chopped green chiles evenly over the Canadian bacon. Sprinkle the Monterey Jack cheese over the chiles.

In a large bowl, beat together the eggs and milk with a mixer. Pour the mixture evenly over the ingredients in the baking dish. Top with the remaining Canadian bacon. Cover with the shredded cheddar cheese. Bake for about 30 minutes. Let the casserole stand 5-10 minutes before serving. Serve with salsa and sour cream.

Blue Skies

B ed and breakfast travelers realize their creative fantasies at the Blue Skies Inn. Whether it's sleeping among fish or beside an ancient Native American sandstone wall, all suites have been designed, painted and tiled by an artist, and offer 10 distinctive themes.

Breakfast is a sumptuous treat that includes an egg dish, freshly baked muffins or pastries, fresh fruit, juice and coffee.

INNKEEPERS:	Sally & Mike
ADDRESS:	402 Manitou Avenue
	Manitou Springs, CO 80829
TELEPHONE:	(719) 685-3899; (800) 398-7949
E-MAIL:	sally@blueskiesbb.com
WEBSITE:	www.blueskiesbb.com
ROOMS:	10 Suites; All with private baths
CHILDREN:	Welcome
ANIMALS:	Not allowed
HANDICAPPED:	Is handicapped accessible
DIETARY NEEDS:	Will accommodate guests' special dietary needs

Green Eggs, No Ham

Makes 2 Large Servings

This is a great breakfast dish for vegetarians. And if there are meat-eating guests at the same meal, you can always serve ham on the side!

5	eggs
1	cup chopped frozen spinach, thawed (partially drained)
¼	cup milk
1	cup soft bread cubes

Salt and pepper to taste

¼	cup shredded Swiss cheese

Fresh chopped tomatoes for garnish

Preheat oven to 375°. Coat an 8x8-inch baking dish with nonstick cooking spray.

In a large bowl, beat the eggs with a fork. Add the spinach, milk, bread cubes, salt and pepper. Stir until thoroughly mixed. Pour mixture into prepared baking dish. Sprinkle the shredded cheese over the top.

Bake for 25 minutes, or until set. Serve garnished with chopped tomatoes.

Maxwell House

Located within walking distance of the shops and restaurants in historic Castle Rock, the Maxwell House Bed and Breakfast features family heirlooms, handmade quilts, pinewood floors and beautiful antiques.

A full breakfast includes entrées such as a green chile torte, German puff pancakes and a custard-topped spoon bread served with pure maple syrup.

INNKEEPERS:	Becky Thomas
ADDRESS:	15 Lewis Street
	Castle Rock, CO 80104
TELEPHONE:	(303) 688-4792
E-MAIL:	info@castlerockbandb.com
WEBSITE:	www.castlerockbandb.com
ROOMS:	2 Rooms; 1 with private bath
CHILDREN:	Call ahead
ANIMALS:	Not allowed
HANDICAPPED:	Not handicapped accessible
DIETARY NEEDS:	Will accommodate guests' special dietary needs

Maxwell House Egg Dish

Makes 8 Servings

This egg specialty, with a Southwestern flair, is delicious served with hot, buttered flour tortillas or muffins. Remember to start preparation a day in advance.

6-8 slices (½- to ¾-inch thick) firm white bread
1-2 tablespoons butter, room temperature
1 (4-ounce) can chopped green chiles
8 eggs
2½ cups milk
½ teaspoon salt, or to taste
1 clove garlic, minced (optional)
3 cups shredded sharp cheddar cheese
3 cups shredded Monterey Jack cheese
Avocado slices for serving
Sour cream for serving
Salsa for serving

Coat a 13x9-inch baking dish with nonstick cooking spray. Cut the crusts off the bread slices. (Use the number of slices it takes to cover the bottom of the baking dish, cutting the slices to fit, if necessary.) Lightly butter the bread; place the slices (butter-side up) in the baking dish. Evenly distribute the green chiles over the bread.

In a large bowl, beat together the eggs, milk, salt and optional garlic. Pour the egg mixture over the bread and chiles. Top with the cheddar and Monterey Jack cheese (the 2 kinds can be mixed together). Cover and refrigerate overnight.

Preheat oven to 350°F. Bake, uncovered, for approximately 50 minutes, or until firm and puffy. Serve with sliced avocado, sour cream and salsa.

Hilltop Inn Guest House

The Hilltop Inn Guest House and Suites is part of a growing gateway community located between historic Boulder and metropolitan Denver. The inn caters primarily to the corporate traveler and specializes in off-site business meetings, whole-facility conferences and special events such as corporate cocktail parties and private catered dinners.

"I travel all over the world, and this is the only place I stay that I actually look forward to." — Guest, Hilltop Inn Guest House

INNKEEPERS:	John Odde
ADDRESS:	9009 Jeffco Airport Avenue
	Broomfield, CO 80021
TELEPHONE:	(303)469-3900; (800) 233-5633
E-MAIL:	info@guest-house.com
WEBSITE:	www.guest-house.com
ROOMS:	2 Rooms; 2 Suites; All with private baths
CHILDREN:	Call ahead
ANIMALS:	Not allowed
HANDICAPPED:	Is handicapped accessible
DIETARY NEEDS:	Will accommodate guests' special dietary needs

Sausage Soufflé

Makes 8 Servings

Assemble the soufflé a day ahead, as the mixture needs to be refrigerated overnight. Serve this wonderful egg dish with slices of colorful melon or any other fruit of choice.

1	pound bulk breakfast sausage
4	cups cubed, day-old bread
2	cups (8 ounces) shredded Monterey Jack or cheddar cheese
10	eggs
4	cups milk
1	teaspoon dry mustard powder
1	teaspoon salt
½	teaspoon nutmeg
½	teaspoon onion powder

Optional ingredients: chopped onions, green pepper, mushrooms, etc.

Coat a 13x9-inch baking dish with butter or nonstick cooking spray. In a skillet, cook the sausage, breaking it up into small pieces. Remove cooked sausage from skillet and drain on paper towels. Place the cubed bread into the bottom of the prepared baking dish. Sprinkle the cheese over the bread.

In a large bowl, beat the eggs. Add the milk, dry mustard, salt, nutmeg and onion powder; mix well. Pour the egg mixture evenly over the bread and cheese. Sprinkle the sausage on top, as well as any of the optional ingredients, if using. Cover; refrigerate overnight.

Preheat oven to 325°F. Bake uncovered for 60-65 minutes. Cover loosely with foil if the top starts to brown. Let stand 10-15 minutes before serving. Cut into squares.

Outlook Lodge

B uilt in 1889 as a parsonage for a neighboring church, the Outlook Lodge has hosted many guests since the early 1950's. Guests enjoy hiking, sightseeing in the Pikes Peak area, skiing, horseback riding or just marveling at the natural sandstone formations in the Garden of the Gods.

The Outlook Lodge Bed and Breakfast is ideally suited for conferences, weddings, reunions, receptions and workshops.

INNKEEPERS:	Diane & Pat Drayton
ADDRESS:	PO Box 586
	Green Mountain Falls, CO 80819
TELEPHONE:	(719) 684-2303
EMAIL:	goofy7@att.net
WEBSITE:	www.outlooklodge.com
ROOMS:	5 Rooms; All with private baths
CHILDREN:	Welcome
ANIMALS:	Not allowed
HANDICAPPED:	Not handicapped accessible
DIETARY NEEDS:	Will accommodate guests' special dietary needs

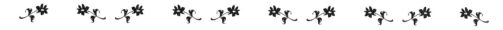

Ham Strata

Makes 8 Servings

12   slices (regular size) white bread
3   cups (12 ounces) shredded cheddar cheese
1   (10-ounce) package frozen chopped broccoli, thawed
2   cups chopped or thinly sliced cooked ham
6   eggs
2½   cups milk
2   tablespoons instant onion
½   teaspoon salt
¼   teaspoon dry mustard
Cheddar cheese, shredded, for garnish

Coat a 13x9-inch baking dish with nonstick cooking spray. Cut a round shape (approximately 3 inches in diameter) from each slice of bread using a cookie cutter or the top of a glass. Set aside the round shapes. Tear the leftover scraps of bread into bite-size pieces and place in bottom of baking dish. Arrange cheese on top of bread scraps. Add a layer of broccoli and then a layer of ham. Place bread circles on top – arrange in 3 rows of 4 bread circles each.

Combine eggs, milk, instant onion, salt and dry mustard and pour over ingredients in the pan, including bread circles. Cover and refrigerate overnight, or for at least 6-8 hours.

Preheat oven to 325°F. Bake uncovered for approximately 60-65 minutes. Sprinkle with some cheddar cheese for the last 5 minutes, and bake until cheese melts. Let stand at least 5 minutes before cutting.

Raindrop

Raindrop Bed and Breakfast would like to give thanks

for all the ways our patrons allow us to grow and be!

Located on 26 acres at the mouth of the Poudre Canyon, Raindrop Bed and Breakfast offers privacy and tranquility in the rolling foothills of the Rocky Mountains. Sports enthusiasts enjoy biking, hiking, fishing, skiing or river rafting.

Guests of the Raindrop Bed and Breakfast experience "a retreat in nature."

INNKEEPERS:	Tara Parr
ADDRESS:	6901 McMurry
	Bellvue, CO 80512
TELEPHONE:	(970) 493-0799
E-MAIL:	None
WEBSITE:	www.bbonline.com/co/raindrop
ROOMS:	3 Rooms; All with private baths
CHILDREN:	Welcome
ANIMALS:	Not allowed
HANDICAPPED:	Partially handicapped accessible; Call ahead
DIETARY NEEDS:	Will accommodate guests' special dietary needs

Chile Rellenos Casserole

Makes 4 to 6 Servings

"This is a very hearty dish! All of our eggs are from our free-range chickens. Our guests see the chickens walk by while they eat breakfast. I love to garden and cook, and I use mainly organic ingredients and home grown veggies." — *Tara Parr, Raindrop B&B*

1	cup crumbled tofu
1	cup shredded Monterey Jack cheese
⅓	cup sliced olives (any kind)
12	Poblano chiles, roasted, or use Anaheim for a milder taste (can be purchased fresh roasted at Farmers' Market and frozen)
4	eggs, separated
3	tablespoons butter, melted and cooled

Sour cream for garnish
Salsa for garnish

Coat an 11x8-inch (or similar size) baking dish with nonstick cooking spray. In a medium bowl, make the filling by mixing the tofu, cheese and olives together. Set aside. Remove the skins and seeds from the roasted chiles. Fill chiles with tofu mixture and place in the baking dish.

Preheat oven to 350°F. Beat egg yolks well and add melted butter. In a separate bowl, beat egg whites until stiff and fold into egg yolk mixture. Pour over chiles. Bake for 40-45 minutes, or until egg mixture is set. Top with sour cream and warm salsa. Serve with rice and beans.

Stonehaven

S tonehaven Bed and Breakfast is a 1906 Victorian home that has been restored to its original glory. The gazebo is an ideal place for weddings, reunions or other gatherings for special occasions. For events with 30 to 125 people, the entire house must be rented for at least the night of the event.

The view of the Colorado National Monument from the Grey Room on the second floor is breathtaking. It's a favorite room for anniversaries.

INNKEEPERS:	Amy Kadrmas
ADDRESS:	798 North Mesa Street
	Fruita, CO 81521
TELEPHONE:	(970) 858-0898; (800) 303-0898
E-MAIL:	amykadrmas@hotmail.com
WEBSITE:	www.stonehavenbed.com
ROOMS:	3 Rooms; 1 Suite; Private & shared baths
CHILDREN:	Well-behaved children are welcome
ANIMALS:	Not allowed; Local kennels board pets
HANDICAPPED:	Not handicapped accessible
DIETARY NEEDS:	Will accommodate guests' special dietary needs

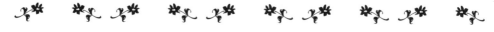

Hearty Breakfast Strata

Makes 6 to 8 Servings

This very filling dish is perfect for big appetites. It's great to serve guests before sending them out for a day on the slopes! The ingredient amounts can vary depending on how many people you are serving and your own individual taste.

1   (32 ounce) bag O'Brien potatoes or hash browns
     (O'Brien potatoes have peppers and onions)
Salsa or taco sauce
Breakfast meat of choice (ham, bacon, sausage, Canadian bacon)
6-8 eggs
Cheddar cheese, shredded or sliced

Fry potatoes in a skillet until done, following package directions. While potatoes are frying, cook meat. Cook eggs over-easy.

Preheat oven to 350°F. Coat a 13x9-inch baking dish with nonstick cooking spray. Assemble strata in baking dish in this order: potatoes, salsa or taco sauce (to your taste), meat, eggs and cheese. Bake for 5-10 minutes, or until cheese melts.

Dripping Springs Inn

Dripping Springs Inn is a unique country inn located in the Roosevelt National Forest on the Big Thompson River. Seven acres of ponderosa pines and aspens allow plenty of wildlife viewing for guests.

Delicious homemade breakfasts are served every morning. "What a wonderful breakfast! As far as baking, Betty Crocker don't have a thing on you all." — a Dripping Springs guest

INNKEEPERS:	Oliver & Janie Robertson
ADDRESS:	2551 Highway 34
	Drake, CO 80515 (Estes Park)
TELEPHONE:	(970) 586-3406; (800) 432-7145
E-MAIL:	innestes@aol.com
WEBSITE:	www.drippingsprings.com
ROOMS:	9 Rooms; Private & shared baths
CHILDREN:	Not allowed
ANIMALS:	Not allowed
HANDICAPPED:	Not handicapped accessible
DIETARY NEEDS:	Will accommodate guests' special dietary needs

Mexicali Sausage & Cheese Bake

Makes 6 to 8 Servings

Get a head start on this easy, flavorful breakfast dish by cooking the sausage in advance. In the morning, all you have left to do is assemble and bake.

1   pound bulk breakfast sausage
2   cans (10-count) refrigerated biscuit dough
1   (8-ounce) jar (1 cup) mild Pace picante sauce
1   cup (4 ounces) shredded cheddar cheese (or cheese of choice)

In a large skillet, crumble and brown the sausage. Drain the sausage on paper towels and set aside to cool. (If cooked ahead, refrigerate the sausage until ready to use.)

Preheat the oven to 350°F Coat an 11x7-inch baking dish with nonstick cooking spray. Separate the biscuit dough into 20 biscuits. Cut each biscuit into 6 pieces and place the pieces in a large bowl. Add the picante sauce and toss lightly. Add the cheese and cooled sausage. Mix gently. Spoon the mixture into the prepared baking dish. Bake for 20-30 minutes. Spoon up and enjoy!

Abriendo Inn

Listed on the National Register of Historic Places, the Abriendo Inn traces its origin to the enterprise of Martin Walter, a German-born brewmaster. After purchasing the Pueblo Brewery in 1898, Mr. Walter hired a California architect to design a brick house for his growing family.

Twenty-seven different brands of beer were produced by his renamed Walter Brewery Company and distributed in seven western states before its closure during the Prohibition Era.

INNKEEPERS:	Kerrelyn Trent
ADDRESS:	300 West Abriendo Avenue
	Pueblo, CO 81004
TELEPHONE:	(719) 544-2703
E-MAIL:	info@abriendoinn.com
WEBSITE:	www.abriendoinn.com
ROOMS:	10 Rooms; All with private baths
CHILDREN:	Children age 7 and older are welcome
ANIMALS:	Not allowed
HANDICAPPED:	Not handicapped accessible
DIETARY NEEDS:	Will accommodate guests' special dietary needs

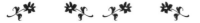

Roasted Red Pepper Eggs

Makes 8 Servings

This colorful egg dish is very popular with guests at Abriendo Inn. In fact, one business traveler who frequently stays there (and in other B&B's almost on a weekly basis) claims that these are her very favorite eggs. Note: This dish needs to refrigerate overnight.

1	cup chopped roasted red chile peppers (about 6-8)
¼	cup freshly grated Parmesan cheese
14	eggs
1	cup milk
½	teaspoon dried basil
½	teaspoon salt
¼	teaspoon pepper
4	ounces cream cheese

Coat a 13x9-inch baking dish with nonstick cooking spray. Distribute the chopped peppers onto the bottom of the pan. Sprinkle with cheese. In a large bowl, beat eggs and milk together, then add the basil, salt and pepper. Mix well. Gently pour the egg mixture over the peppers and cheese (the peppers and cheese will rise to the top). Cover and refrigerate overnight.

The next morning, preheat oven to 350°F. Bake, uncovered, for 45-50 minutes, or until eggs are set. Note: The recipe can be cut in half and baked in an 8x8-inch baking pan for approximately 30 minutes.

> **Carol's Corner**
> *Chiles can be roasted in the oven, but they can also be purchased roasted at Farmers' Markets or in grocery stores packed in jars or cans. For a real chile experience, attend the annual Chile & Frijoles Festival in Pueblo, Colorado. Every September, the town celebrates the harvest of the Pueblo chiles with authentic food, music and an 1840's historical market. Festival-goers can purchase roasted chiles in large quantities and freeze them at home in recipe-size portions for year-round convenience.*

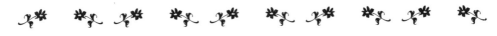

Pikes Peak Paradise

The four guest suites featured at the Pikes Peak Paradise Bed and Breakfast boast distinctive, luxurious accommodations that offer romance, quiet elegance and spaciousness. Located northwest of Colorado Springs in Woodland Park, all rooms have majestic views of Pikes Peak.

Amenities include in-room hot tubs and fireplaces, a hearty breakfast and complimentary beverages and snacks.

INNKEEPERS:	Rayne & Bart Reese
ADDRESS:	236 Pinecrest Road
	Woodland Park, CO 80863
TELEPHONE:	(719) 687-6656
E-MAIL:	pppbnb@bemail.com
WEBSITE:	www.pikespeakmall.com/pppbandb
ROOMS:	1 Room; 4 Suites; Private & shared baths
CHILDREN:	Children age 10 and older are welcome
ANIMALS:	Well-behaved dogs are welcome; Resident cats
HANDICAPPED:	Not handicapped accessible
DIETARY NEEDS:	Will accommodate guests' special dietary needs

Paradise Egg Dish

Makes 1 or More Servings

Serving one guest? Two guests? Six guests? No problem! This breakfast dish is baked and served in individual dishes, and the ingredients can be multiplied to accommodate the number of guests or family members you are serving.

1	slice of bacon, cut into pieces
2	eggs
¼	cup milk
½	teaspoon chopped green chiles
1	teaspoon cottage cheese
1	tablespoon sour cream
2	slices cheese (use 1 slice each of two different kinds, such as cheddar and Monterey Jack)

Preheat oven to 325°F. Coat individual 8x4x1½-inch oval baking dishes (or similar 1-cup capacity dish) with nonstick cooking spray.

In a skillet, cook the bacon pieces until crisp; drain on paper towels. Drain the bacon grease from skillet, reserving ½ teaspoon. In a bowl, whisk together the eggs and milk. Return the reserved bacon grease to the skillet and add the egg mixture. Lightly scramble the eggs until partially done. Add the green chiles and cottage cheese; mix thoroughly. Spoon mixture into prepared baking dish.

Spread the sour cream over the top of the eggs. Sprinkle with the bacon pieces. Place the slices of cheese over the top.

Bake eggs for 10-15 minutes, or until the cheese is melted and the eggs are heated through.

Lightner Creek Inn

The Lightner Creek Inn, located on 20 pristine acres with a duck pond and stream, offers a casual, yet elegant romantic escape. Guests enjoy the privacy of the Carriage House (a 700 square foot studio) or any of the other rooms, all furnished with down comforters and antique furniture.

In winter, guests can enjoy Nordic or Alpine skiing, experience a dinner sleigh ride or simply sit by a cozy fire.

INNKEEPERS:	Suzy & Stan Savage
ADDRESS:	999 C.R. 207
	Durango, CO 81301
TELEPHONE:	(970) 259-1226
E-MAIL:	lci@frontier.net
WEBSITE:	www.lightnercreekinn.com
ROOMS:	10 Rooms; 3 Suites; All with private baths
CHILDREN:	Children age 5 and older are welcome
ANIMALS:	Not allowed
HANDICAPPED:	Is handicapped accessible
DIETARY NEEDS:	Will accommodate guests' special dietary needs

Huevos Durangos

Makes 8 Servings

This ham, Swiss cheese and egg casserole can be baked right after preparing, or it can be made in advance and refrigerated for up to 24 hours. When Lightner Creek Inn makes this specialty for their guests, they bake and serve it in individual casserole dishes. Cooking time is reduced to 12-15 minutes.

8	slices French bread, torn into bite-size pieces
2-3	Roma (plum) tomatoes, chopped
3	tablespoons chopped onion
1	cup (about 6 ounces) ground, cooked Black Forest ham
1	cup (4 ounces) shredded Swiss cheese
16	eggs
1	cup half & half
2	(15-ounce) cans Stokes green chile sauce with pork

Preheat oven to 350°F. Coat a 13x9-inch glass baking dish with nonstick cooking spray. Place the torn pieces of bread in the bottom of the dish. Sprinkle the tomato, onion, ground ham (a food processor works well) and shredded cheese over the bread.

In a large bowl, combine the eggs and half & half; mix well. Pour the mixture over the ingredients in the baking dish.

Bake, uncovered, for 40-50 minutes, or until firm. Increase the baking time (about 5-10 minutes), if the dish is coming directly from the refrigerator. Do not overcook or the eggs will be dry.

Heat the green chile sauce. Cut the casserole into squares and serve immediately, topped with the green chile sauce, or serve the sauce in a side dish.

> *✳ Carol's Corner*
> *Stokes is a Colorado company that has been around since 1906. In addition to the zesty green chile sauce used in this recipe, Stokes makes several other excellent chiles and sauces. Their products can be found in most grocery stores.*

Hughes Hacienda

Hughes Hacienda sits high on a hill at the foot of Blue Mountain, outside of Colorado Springs. Guests enjoy magnificent views of the Rocky Mountains, Red Rock Valley and the twinkling of evening lights of Colorado Springs.

Abundant wildlife inhabits the secluded 19 acre hideaway, including deer, raccoon, fox and birds. Guests can hike the well-maintained trails or simply relax in the portal overlooking the mountains and valley below.

INNKEEPERS:	Wayne & Carol Hughes
ADDRESS:	12060 Calle Corvo
	Colorado Springs, CO 80926
TELEPHONE:	(719) 576-2060; (800) 576-2060
E-MAIL:	hugheshacienda@msn.com
WEBSITE:	www.hugheshacienda.com
ROOMS:	1 Suite; Private bath; 1 Room; Adjoining bath
CHILDREN:	Call Ahead
ANIMALS:	Not allowed
HANDICAPPED:	Not handicapped accessible
DIETARY NEEDS:	Will accommodate guests' special dietary needs

Breakfast Rellenos

Makes 2 Servings

4	Anaheim chiles (also called New Mexico #6)
2	tablespoons raw piñon nuts
4	eggs
2	tablespoons golden raisins
½	cup sour cream
1	cup (4 ounces) shredded farmer's cheese
8	slices avocado for garnish

Preheat broiler. Place chiles on a foil-covered cookie sheet. Place 4-6 inches below the broiler unit. Roast chiles for 6-8 minutes, rotating occasionally, until lightly charred and uniformly blistered. Remove from the broiler and place in a paper bag. Close tightly and steam for 5 minutes. Remove from bag and rinse under cold water to remove the skin. Leave the stems on. Make a slit lengthwise in the chile and remove the seeds. Pat dry with paper towel and place on an oven-proof plate, slit side up.

Gently toast piñon nuts in a small iron skillet over low heat until light brown, stirring often to prevent scorching. Scramble the eggs with piñon nuts and raisins. Spoon egg mixture into the prepared chiles. Spoon sour cream over eggs and sprinkle cheese on top. Place under the broiler until cheese melts. Place on serving dish and garnish with avocado slices. Serve with hash brown potatoes, a meat and an assortment of fresh fruit.

Carol's Corner
Farmer's cheese is a soft, very mild white cheese with a wonderful, delicate flavor! Most supermarkets have it available in the deli section. If you are unable to find it, substitute Monterey Jack or Havarti. Wayne Hughes, owner and chef at Hughes Hacienda, has quite a flair when it comes to Mexican food. His combinations of taste, texture and color are sensational.

$\mathcal{TLC}$'s

According to owner Mary Jo Coulehan, TLC does not stand for "Tender Loving Care." It stands for the initials of her parents, Tom and Lottie Coulehan. Mary Jo lost them both within a short period of time. Since they loved the outdoors and traveling, Mary Jo thought it appropriate to name her dream after them.

When Mary Jo bought the house, Ayla, a dog, came with the purchase. Ayla's loving nature has helped one small girl get over her fear of dogs.

INNKEEPERS:	Mary Jo Coulehan
ADDRESS:	PO Box 3337
	Pagosa Springs, CO 81147
TELEPHONE:	(970) 264-6200; (800) 788-5090
E-MAIL:	tlc@pagosa.net
WEBSITE:	www.pagosa.net/tlc
ROOMS:	1 Room; 3 Suites; All with private baths
CHILDREN:	Welcome
ANIMALS:	Not allowed; Call ahead for horse boarding
HANDICAPPED:	Not handicapped accessible
DIETARY NEEDS:	Will accommodate guests' special dietary needs

Scrambled Eggs with Herb Cheese

Makes 4 Servings

"The great treat of this recipe is that it is super easy, great for a 'pop-up' breakfast and most of the items you already have on hand. I get rave reviews on the cream cheese mixture – it's much better than what you can buy in the store, and it's so easy to make. In addition, this recipe can be adjusted to fit the number of people that you are serving. Enjoy!" — Mary Jo Coulehan, TLC's

2	ounces cream cheese
1-2	teaspoons dried basil
Pinch of thyme	
8	eggs
2	tablespoons milk, more if needed
1-2	tablespoons butter or margarine

Optional: chopped onions, mushrooms, green chiles, ham, etc.

In a small bowl, mix cream cheese, basil and thyme. In a medium bowl, scramble eggs and add milk.

In a large skillet, melt the butter. Sauté any of the optional ingredients, depending on your guests' tastes. Add the eggs and cook. When almost fully cooked, add the cream cheese mixture and cook until the cream cheese has melted and is thoroughly combined with the eggs. Serve immediately.

Beddin' Down

Located on a 24 acre ranch, the Beddin' Down Bed, Breakfast and Horse Hotel is a lodge-style log home with facilities for pets and horses. The spectacular Rocky Mountains surround this quiet ranch, providing the setting for outdoor recreation including golf, fishing, mountain biking, hiking, downhill skiing, snowmobiling, ghost town jeep tours, Arkansas River whitewater rafting and cross-country skiing.

Hunting and fishing guides are also available upon request.

INNKEEPERS:	Carolyn & Jerry Sparkman
ADDRESS:	10401 County Road 160
	Salida, CO 81201
TELEPHONE:	(719) 539-1815; (800) 470-1888
E-MAIL:	carolyn@beddindown.com
WEBSITE:	www.beddindown.com
ROOMS:	5 Rooms; All with private baths
CHILDREN:	Welcome
ANIMALS:	Permitted outside only; Resident dogs
HANDICAPPED:	Not handicapped accessible
DIETARY NEEDS:	Will accommodate guests' special dietary needs

Texas Scramble

Makes 4 to 6 Servings

This Southwestern breakfast dish becomes even more special when served with fresh pico de gallo (recipe below) and warm tortilla chips.

12 ounces fresh bulk breakfast sausage
Butter for skillet (about 2 tablespoons)
1 cup (total) mixed, chopped red & green bell pepper
½ cup chopped green onions (save some long green tops for garnish)
6 eggs
½ cup milk
2 red potatoes (microwave until tender, cut into small dice)
½ cup salsa (or to taste)
Warm tortillas
Shredded Mexican-style cheese
Pico de gallo for serving (recipe follows)
Warm tortilla chips, for serving

In a medium skillet, brown the sausage until cooked; drain and set aside. In a large skillet, melt the butter and sauté the peppers and onions. In a medium bowl, beat the eggs and milk. Add the egg mixture to the peppers and onions; scramble until fluffy. Add the potatoes, sausage and salsa. Place a warm tortilla on each plate. Spoon eggs on top and sprinkle with cheese. Garnish with the onion tops. Serve with pico de gallo and tortilla chips.

Pico de gallo:
1 small onion, chopped
1 tomato, chopped
1 jalapeño pepper (or less), seeded and chopped
1 serrano pepper, seeded and chopped
1 tomatillo (Mexican green tomato), papery husk removed and chopped
2 teaspoons fresh lime juice, or more to taste
2 tablespoons chopped fresh cilantro

Mix all ingredients together in a bowl. Season to taste with salt. Pico de gallo can be made ahead and refrigerated overnight.

Evans House

Built in 1886, the Evans House Bed and Breakfast is listed on the National Historic Register. Located in the idyllic mountain town of Breckenridge, this restored Victorian house was once home to the W. H. Evans Pharmacy. Medicinal bottles, photos and relics – that were discovered on-site – decorate the interior walls.

A delicious breakfast includes crêpes, Belgian waffles, apple cinnamon French toast and egg dishes.

INNKEEPERS:	Peter & Georgette Contos
ADDRESS:	102 South French Street
	Breckenridge, CO 80424
TELEPHONE:	(970) 453-5509
E-MAIL:	evans15@mindspring.com
WEBSITE:	www.coloradoevanshouse.com
ROOMS:	6 Rooms; 2 Suites; All with private baths
CHILDREN:	Welcome
ANIMALS:	Not allowed
HANDICAPPED:	Limited accessibility
DIETARY NEEDS:	Will accommodate guests' special dietary needs

Bacon Rings

Makes 6 Servings

A unique twist on traditional eggs Benedict.

12   slices bacon
12   eggs
Garlic powder (about ½ teaspoon)
Dill (about ½ teaspoon)
1   cup (4 ounces) shredded cheddar cheese
Hollandaise sauce for serving (can use a mix)
6   large croissants

Preheat oven to 400°F. Coat a 12-count muffin pan with nonstick cooking spray.

In a large skillet, fry bacon until almost crisp. Drain the slices briefly on paper towels; then quickly place bacon slices in a circle around the inside edge of each muffin cup (this step must be done while the bacon is still warm and pliable). Break an egg into each muffin cup. Sprinkle with garlic powder and dill. Top with cheese.

Bake for 12-20 minutes, depending on desired doneness of eggs. To serve, place two bacon rings on each plate and top with warm hollandaise sauce.

Note: The croissants can be cut in half and served under the bacon rings and sauce, or left whole and served on the side.

Ellen's

Veteran travelers and those with dreams of faraway places will enjoy visiting with innkeepers Baldwin "Baldy" and Ellen Ranson at Ellen's. The Ransons lived for several years in both Korea and Japan where Baldy taught economics and Ellen taught English.

The Ransons often host newlyweds who arrive in "decorated" cars. During breakfast, they watch Innkeeper Baldy out in the yard washing their cars as an added amenity!

INNKEEPERS:	Baldwin & Ellen Ranson
ADDRESS:	700 Kimbark Street
	Longmont, CO 80501
TELEPHONE:	(303) 776-1676
E-MAIL:	ellen@ellensbandb.com
WEBSITE:	www.ellensbandb.com
ROOMS:	2 Rooms; Private baths
CHILDREN:	Welcome
ANIMALS:	Permitted; Resident pets
HANDICAPPED:	Not handicapped accessible
DIETARY NEEDS:	Will accommodate guests' special dietary needs

Fluffy Stuffers

Makes 1 Serving (Multiply as Needed)

An impressive presentation and easy preparation. For variety, try using ham, or leave the meat out altogether and use several different vegetables to please your vegetarian friends.

1	croissant

Butter for skillet

2	eggs, lightly beaten
1	thin slice Swiss cheese
1-2	thin slices turkey
2	fresh asparagus spears (parboiled for 1 minute)

Hollandaise sauce (can use Knorr's mix)
Dash cayenne pepper

Preheat oven to 225°F. Slice croissant in half lengthwise. Wrap in foil and warm in oven.

In a skillet, melt the butter and softly scramble the eggs. Open croissant and on bottom half, gently pile egg, a slice of cheese and a slice of turkey. Crisscross 2 asparagus spears on top. Put the top half on to close the croissant. Wrap in foil.

Put foil "package" in the oven for about 5 minutes to melt cheese. Remove from oven and foil, and place croissant on heated plate. Top with hot Hollandaise sauce. Sprinkle with a dash of cayenne to give it some zing! Add a side of 2 or 3 sliced fresh fruits.

Hughes Hacienda

The comfort and spaciousness of Hughes Hacienda make it the ideal get-away. The Southwestern decor, complete with beamed ceilings, Mexican tile and a kiva-style fireplace, casts a spell on the guests.

The Hacienda has one suite that is furnished with a fireplace, sitting area with library, stereo, TV, wet bar, refrigerator and microwave oven. A gourmet breakfast is served each morning in the privacy of the suite or on the portal overlooking the mountains and valley.

INNKEEPERS:	Wayne & Carol Hughes
ADDRESS:	12060 Calle Corvo
	Colorado Springs, CO 80926
TELEPHONE:	(719) 576-2060; (800) 576-2060
E-MAIL:	hugheshacienda@msn.com
WEBSITE:	www.hugheshacienda.com
ROOMS:	1 Suite; Private bath; 1 Room; Adjoining bath
CHILDREN:	Call Ahead
ANIMALS:	Not allowed
HANDICAPPED:	Not handicapped accessible
DIETARY NEEDS:	Will accommodate guests' special dietary needs

Breakfast Enchiladas

Makes 1 Large or 2 Small Servings

Serve with an assortment of fresh fruit, a meat and hash brown potatoes or pinto beans.

2	tablespoons butter
1	heaping tablespoon flour
¾	cup chicken broth
½	cup milk

Salt and pepper to taste

1	serrano chile pepper, seeded and finely minced
2	eggs
¼	cup chopped zucchini
¼	cup chopped tomato
1	tablespoon pepitas (pumpkin seeds), lightly toasted
2	corn tortillas
½	cup shredded farmer's cheese
4	slices avocado for garnish

Make a white sauce by melting the butter over medium heat and stirring in the flour to form a paste. Add the chicken broth, milk, salt and pepper. Stir constantly until it bubbles and thickens. Stir in the chile pepper and simmer on low heat while preparing the rest of the dish.

Scramble the eggs with diced zucchini, tomato and pumpkin seeds. Pat the tortillas with wet hands to moisten and place on a preheated grill or skillet, turning after 30 seconds. Heat on the second side for 30-40 seconds.

Place tortillas on a serving plate and spoon the cooked egg mixture down the center of each tortilla, rolling the tortillas around the eggs and rotating so the seam side is down. Pour the white sauce over the enchiladas and sprinkle with cheese. Garnish with avocado slices.

Meadow Creek

ASABATTLES

Meadow Creek, once part of the 250 acre Douglass ranch, was built in 1929 by Prince Balthasar Gialma Odescalchi, noble of the Holy Roman Empire. The property is nestled in a secluded meadow surrounded by stone outcroppings. Tall pines and aspens border a small spring-fed creek.

"We are pleased to share our little piece of God's Country." — Owners, Loren & Ivan Fuentes

INNKEEPERS:	Loren & Ivan Fuentes
ADDRESS:	13438 U.S. Highway 285
	Pine, CO 80470
TELEPHONE:	(303) 838-4167; (303) 838-4899
E-MAIL:	info@meadowcreekbb.com
WEBSITE:	www.meadowcreekbb.com
ROOMS:	5 Rooms; 2 Suites; All with private baths
CHILDREN:	Call ahead
ANIMALS:	Not allowed
HANDICAPPED:	Not handicapped accessible
DIETARY NEEDS:	Will accommodate guests' special dietary needs

Ham Quiche Biscuit Cups

Makes 10 Servings

1	(8-ounce) package cream cheese, softened
2	tablespoons milk
2	eggs
½	cup shredded Swiss cheese
2	tablespoons chopped green onion
1	can (10-count) refrigerated flaky biscuits
½	cup finely chopped ham

Preheat oven to 375°F. Grease 10 muffin cups. Beat cream cheese, milk and eggs until smooth. Stir in Swiss cheese and green onions.

Separate dough into 10 biscuits. Place one biscuit in each cup. Firmly press in bottom and up sides, forming a ¼-inch rim. Place half of ham in bottom of dough cups. Spoon about 2 tablespoons cheese and egg mixture over ham. Top with remaining ham.

Bake for about 25 minutes, or until filling is set and edges of biscuits are golden brown. Remove from pan. Serve immediately.

Alps Boulder Canon Inn

The common areas of the Alps Boulder Canyon Inn are furnished in the warm and homey-style of the great lodges and camps of the northeastern United States. Built in the 1870's, the lounge has been converted into a social area where guests can meet, converse and relax in an authentic turn-of-the-twentieth-century mountain lodge.

The entrance area is the original log cabin.

INNKEEPERS:	John & Jeannine Vanderhart
ADDRESS:	38619 Boulder Canyon Drive
	Boulder, CO 80302
TELEPHONE:	(303) 444-5445
E-MAIL:	info@alpsinn.com
WEBSITE:	www.alpsinn.com
ROOMS:	12 Rooms; All with private baths
CHILDREN:	Children age 12 and older are welcome
ANIMALS:	Not allowed; Resident dog
HANDICAPPED:	Not handicapped accessible
DIETARY NEEDS:	Will accommodate guests' special dietary needs

San Juan Soufflé

Makes 10 Large Servings

This is a great make-ahead recipe, as the soufflé mixture will keep in the refrigerator for several days, or may even be frozen. Another plus, because the soufflé is baked in individual dishes, you can bake as many or as few servings as you need at a time. Beware – jalapeño peppers give this superb dish quite a kick! The Alps Boulder Canyon Inn suggests serving the soufflé with cornbread.

½	cup (1 stick) butter
10	eggs
4	cups (16 ounces) shredded cheddar cheese
4	cups (32 ounces) small curd cottage cheese
½	cup all-purpose flour
1	teaspoon baking powder
1	(4-ounce) can diced green chiles
1	(4-ounce) can diced jalapeños (red or green)
½	cup diced red bell pepper
½	cup diced onion

Melt the butter and set aside to cool. In a large bowl, beat the egg well. Combine eggs with the cheeses, flour, baking powder, green chiles, jalapenos, red pepper and onion. Mix well. If not baking immediately, cover and store in the refrigerator (or freeze).

To bake, preheat oven to 400°F. Grease large individual ramekins or baking dishes (1 cup capacity or slightly larger) and spoon nearly 1 cup of the soufflé mixture into each. Bake about 25-30 minutes, or until the top is golden and the middle is firm.

Note: If desired, this recipe can easily be cut in half.

Leadville Country Inn

Guests of the Leadville Country Inn enjoy local activities that include following the route of the Silver Kings, with a drive through the fabled mining district, or touring the historic Matchless Mine.

The on-going renovation of many structures in Leadville's National Historic District, such as the Tabor Opera House, are a testimony to the tenacity of local citizens to preserve this piece of history, when Leadville was the most prosperous of Colorado's 1880's boom towns.

INNKEEPERS:	Maureen & Gretchen Scanlon
ADDRESS:	127 East 8th Street
	Leadville, CO 80461
TELEPHONE:	(719) 486-2354
E-MAIL:	lcinn@bemail.com
WEBSITE:	www.leadvillebednbreakfast.com
ROOMS:	8 Rooms; All with private baths
CHILDREN:	Children age 10 and older are welcome
ANIMALS:	Not allowed
HANDICAPPED:	Not handicapped accessible
DIETARY NEEDS:	Will accommodate guests' special dietary needs

Cloud City Apple & Brie Omelette

Makes 2 Servings

This omelette is a winning combination of tastes and textures. Complete the meal with toasted sourdough bread or savory bagels.

1   tablespoon butter
1   Granny Smith apple, peeled, cored and thinly sliced
⅛   teaspoon nutmeg
1   teaspoon white sugar
1   tablespoon brown sugar
2   tablespoons chopped walnuts
3   eggs
¼   cup skim milk
Small cubes of Brie cheese
Spiced apple rings for garnish, chilled

In a small skillet, melt the butter; sauté the apple slices until glassy, but not mushy. Sprinkle the apple slices with the nutmeg and white sugar; stir to combine. Remove from heat and set aside.

In a small dish, mix the brown sugar and walnuts; set aside. In a medium bowl, beat together the eggs and milk.

Coat a 6 to 8-inch nonstick skillet or omelette pan with nonstick cooking spray (or butter). Heat the pan over medium heat; pour the egg mixture into the skillet and gently cook. As the eggs start to set, lift edges of omelette to allow uncooked mixture to seep underneath. When eggs are set, turn off heat and place Brie cubes on half of the omelette. Top with sautéed apple slices. Cover the skillet and let the omelette stand for 3-4 minutes to melt the Brie.

Slide the omelette from the pan onto a plate, folding the portion of the omelette without cheese and apples over the other half. Sprinkle the top of the omelette with the brown sugar and walnut mixture. Cut omelette in half for 2 servings. Garnish the plates with chilled, spiced apple rings.

Woodland Inn

Woodland Inn is a cozy country inn nestled in the foothills of majestic Pikes Peak. Surrounded by 12 acres of aspen and fir trees, the inn is conveniently located just minutes from Colorado Springs and Manitou Springs in beautiful Woodland Park, truly "The City Above the Clouds."

Hot air balloon flights can be arranged for a morning of adventure. "A special, unexpected treasure," one guest commented. "We'll remember this forever."

INNKEEPERS:	Frank & Susan Gray
ADDRESS:	159 Trull Road
	Woodland Park, CO 80863
TELEPHONE:	(719) 687-8209; (800) 226-9565
E-MAIL:	woodlandinn@aol.com
WEBSITE:	www.woodlandinn.com
ROOMS:	7 Rooms; All with private baths
CHILDREN:	Welcome
ANIMALS:	Not allowed; Resident dog and cat
HANDICAPPED:	Not handicapped accessible
DIETARY NEEDS:	Will accommodate guests' special dietary needs

Frank's Seafood Omelette

Makes 4 Servings

The combination of flavors is perfect! An impressive dish! Serve with fresh fruit and hot muffins. Makes 4 (2 egg) omelettes. You can also make 1 egg omelettes and reduce the filling accordingly.

2	tablespoons butter
8	green onions, chopped
2	cups sliced fresh mushrooms
1	dozen shrimp, medium size, cooked and halved lengthwise (set aside 4 halves for garnish)
8	ounces crab meat, cooked (or imitation crab)
½	cup sour cream
8	eggs (2 per omelette)
1-2	cups shredded Swiss cheese

Parsley for garnish

Melt butter in skillet and sauté onions and mushrooms until soft. Add cooked seafood (setting aside 4 shrimp halves to be used for garnish). Add sour cream. Stir together, warm over very low temperature and set aside (do not allow sour cream to boil).

Whip eggs (2 at a time) and pour into a buttered 8-inch omelette pan over medium-high heat. Lift edges frequently to allow uncooked portion to flow underneath. Sprinkle ¼-½ cup cheese over center portion of omelette. Lower heat to medium, cover and cook for 1-2 minutes. Add ½ cup seafood mixture on top of one half of omelette. Cover and cook until egg mixture is set, about 2 minutes.

Fold omelette over seafood portion and slide omelette onto a warm plate. Keep warm in a 200°F oven while preparing the remaining omelettes. Garnish top with halved shrimp and a sprig of parsley.

Beddin' Down

L ocated approximately 10 miles west of Salida, the Beddin' Down Bed, Breakfast and Horse Hotel offers lodging and accommodations in a beautiful lodge-style cabin with facilities for pets and horses.

"There is a reason we love to keep coming back. Y'all make us feel like family. That's the same reason it is hard to leave." — Guest, Beddin' Down

INNKEEPERS:	Carolyn & Jerry Sparkman
ADDRESS:	10401 County Road 160
	Salida, CO 81201
TELEPHONE:	(719) 539-1815; (800) 470-1888
E-MAIL:	carolyn@beddindown.com
WEBSITE:	www.beddindown.com
ROOMS:	5 Rooms; All with private baths
CHILDREN:	Welcome
ANIMALS:	Permitted outside only; Resident dogs
HANDICAPPED:	Not handicapped accessible
DIETARY NEEDS:	Will accommodate guests' special dietary needs

Stuffed Breakfast Croissants

Makes 8 Servings

These triangle-shaped breakfast pastries are terrific. Fresh fruit or avocado slices make a nice complement to the meal.

8   eggs
½   cup milk
Garlic pepper to taste (or other seasoning of choice)
Chopped cilantro to taste
1   teaspoon dry mustard powder
Butter for skillet
1   cup shredded Mexican-style cheese (plus more for garnish)
2   (8-ounce) cans refrigerated Pillsbury crescent rolls
4   thin slices lean ham
8   tablespoons sour cream for garnish
Salsa for garnish
Chopped green onions for garnish

Preheat oven to 375°F. In a large bowl, combine eggs, milk, garlic pepper, cilantro and mustard. Whisk until well blended. In a large non-stick skillet, scramble the egg mixture in a small amount of butter. When the eggs are done, cover them with 1 cup of cheese; let sit to allow cheese to melt.

On an ungreased cookie sheet, carefully unroll one can of crescent rolls. Separate the rolls into 4 rectangular pieces by leaving the rolls together by two's (gently push the two rolls together along the perforation line). Place a slice of ham over each of the 4 pieces of dough and cover each with ¼ of the eggs and cheese. Unroll the remaining can of rolls. Separate into 4 rectangles, as above. Place the dough over the filling to form a top for the 4 pastries. Crimp the top and bottom edges of the dough together, using either a fork or your fingers, to seal the pastries.

Bake for 15-20 minutes, until golden brown. To serve, slice each pastry along the perforation line into two triangles. Garnish each serving with a dollop of sour cream, salsa and a sprinkling of chopped green onions and shredded cheese.

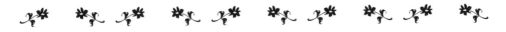

Room at the Inn

In addition to being a luxurious bed and breakfast, the Room at the Inn offers beautiful and functional surroundings for corporate events, small weddings, receptions, rehearsal dinners, bridal luncheons, anniversary gatherings, elegant birthday parties and other special celebrations.

Located in a Victorian neighborhood near downtown Colorado Springs, this charming inn is a short stroll to unique restaurants and shops.

INNKEEPERS:	Dorian & Linda Ciolek
ADDRESS:	618 North Nevada Avenue
	Colorado Springs, CO 80903
TELEPHONE:	(719) 442-1896; (888) 442-1896
E-MAIL:	roomatinn@pcisys.net
WEBSITE:	www.roomattheinn.com
ROOMS:	8 Rooms; All with private baths
CHILDREN:	Children age 12 and older are welcome
ANIMALS:	Not allowed
HANDICAPPED:	Is handicapped accessible
DIETARY NEEDS:	Will accommodate guests' special dietary needs

Farmer's Breakfast

Makes 5 to 6 Servings

Potatoes, ham and eggs, all in one delectable dish! A sweet, fruity muffin or a piece of streusel-topped coffee cake would be a welcome addition to this hearty quiche. Tip: Put the hash browns in the refrigerator overnight to thaw between layers of paper towels, and they'll be ready to go in the morning.

15   ounces (about 4½ cups) frozen hash browns (any style), thawed
Spray butter or about 2 tablespoons melted butter
8   eggs
1   cup half & half
1   teaspoon chervil (or dried parsley)
1   teaspoon chopped chives (dried or fresh)
½   teaspoon salt
½   teaspoon white pepper
2   cups (8 ounces) shredded colby cheese
6   ounces (about 1 cup) Canadian bacon or ham, chopped
Tomato slices for garnish
Cilantro sprigs for garnish

Preheat oven to 400°F. Coat a 9-inch deep-dish pie plate with nonstick cooking spray. Press thawed hash browns between paper towels to remove excess moisture. Place hash browns into the prepared pie plate and press to form an even, solid crust on the bottom and sides of the pie plate. Spray potatoes evenly with spray butter, or brush with melted butter. Bake the potato crust for 20 minutes.

Meanwhile, in a large bowl, beat together the eggs, half & half, chervil, chives, salt and pepper. After removing the potato crust from the oven, sprinkle the cheese on top of the potatoes and cover with the Canadian bacon or ham. Give the egg mixture another stir to thoroughly mix the ingredients, and pour over all ingredients in the pie plate.

Lower oven temperature to 350°F. Bake for 45 minutes, or until set. Let quiche stand for about 10 minutes before slicing. Garnish plates with sliced tomatoes and sprigs of cilantro.

Lavender Swing

Nestled at the foot of the magnificent Rocky Mountains, the Lavender Swing Bed and Breakfast of Glenwood Springs boasts three lovely and spacious upstairs rooms with queen-size beds and private baths. Each room offers antique charm and quiet comfort.

Area activities include snowshoeing, skiing, hiking, biking, cross-country skiing or a scenic drive to nearby Aspen for shopping and fine dining.

INNKEEPERS:	Pat Means & Carolyn Goller
ADDRESS:	802 Palmer Avenue
	Glenwood Springs, CO 81601
TELEPHONE:	(970) 945-8289
E-MAIL:	lavender@rof.net
WEBSITE:	www.lavenderswing.com
ROOMS:	3 Rooms; All with private baths
CHILDREN:	Children age 15 and older are welcome
ANIMALS:	Not allowed; Resident parrot "Sally"
HANDICAPPED:	Not handicapped accessible
DIETARY NEEDS:	Will accommodate guests' special dietary needs

Rice Crust Quiche

Makes 6 Servings

1	cup wild rice or brown rice, cooked and cooled (about 3 cups cooked rice)
1	tablespoon butter
¼	cup diced green onion
¼	cup diced red bell pepper
½	cup chopped ham (or use ½ cup more diced vegetables)
1	cup (4 ounces) shredded Swiss cheese
4	eggs
½	cup milk
¼	cup sour cream
1	tablespoon dried basil
¼	teaspoon garlic powder
¼	teaspoon salt

Sour cream for topping
Salsa for topping

Preheat oven to 350°F. Coat a 10-inch quiche dish or pie plate with nonstick cooking spray. Cook rice according to package directions with the butter. Set aside to cool. (The rice can be made the night before and refrigerated.)

Spoon the cooked and cooled rice into the prepared dish. Press the rice evenly around the dish and up the sides with a wooden spoon to form a crust. Sprinkle the green onion, red pepper, ham and half of the cheese onto the bottom of the crust.

In a medium bowl, beat together the eggs, milk, sour cream, basil, garlic powder and salt. Pour the egg mixture over all of the ingredients in the dish. Sprinkle the remaining cheese over the top. Bake for 45 minutes. Let stand 5-10 minutes before slicing. Serve topped with sour cream or salsa.

Husted House

Situated on a shady corner in Old Colorado Springs, the Husted House Bed and Breakfast was originally the residence of one of Colorado's most successful entrepreneurs. This beautiful Victorian Gothic home is located near charming shops and quaint streets at the foothills of the magnificent Rocky Mountains.

Area attractions include Garden of the Gods, Pro Rodeo Hall of Fame, World Figure Skating Museum, Air Force Academy and Pikes Peak.

INNKEEPERS:	Shirley & Clint Waller
ADDRESS:	3001 West Kiowa Street
	Colorado Springs, CO 80904
TELEPHONE:	(719) 632-7569
E-MAIL:	Husted1894@cs.com
WEBSITE:	www.avenetmkt.com/husted
ROOMS:	2 Rooms; Private baths
CHILDREN:	Call ahead
ANIMALS:	Not allowed
HANDICAPPED:	Is handicapped accessible
DIETARY NEEDS:	Will accommodate guests' special dietary needs

Aunt Norma's Swiss Pie

Makes 4 to 6 Servings

Accompany this delicious quiche with a colorful bowl of fresh peach slices and red raspberries.

1	cup fine cracker crumbs (26 saltines)
¼	cup (½ stick) butter, melted
6	slices bacon
½	cup chopped onion
2	eggs
¾	cup sour cream
½	teaspoon salt

Dash of pepper

2	cups (8 ounces) shredded Swiss cheese
½	cup (2 ounces) shredded sharp processed cheese

Chives (the slender hollow stems) for garnish

Preheat oven to 375°F. Coat an 8-inch pie plate with nonstick cooking spray. Combine cracker crumbs and melted butter. Form a crust by pressing the crumb mixture firmly and evenly into the bottom and up the sides of the pie plate.

In a large skillet, cook the bacon until crisp. Reserve 2 tablespoons of the bacon fat. Drain and cool the cooked bacon on paper towels. Crumble the bacon when cool and set aside. Sauté the chopped onion in the reserved bacon fat until transparent, but do not brown it.

In a medium bowl, slightly beat the eggs. Mix in the crumbled bacon, onion, sour cream, salt, pepper and Swiss cheese. Pour the mixture into the crust. Sprinkle the shredded processed cheese evenly over the top.

Bake for 25-30 minutes, or until a knife inserted halfway between the center and edge of the quiche comes out clean, and the top is nicely browned. Let stand 10-15 minutes before cutting into serving pieces. Garnish each piece with "swords" of chive.

Derby Hill Inn

Guests of the Derby Hill Inn Bed and Breakfast experience a restful night's sleep, with such in-room amenities as plush robes and fresh flowers. Fax and computer with Internet access are available at no charge.

Loveland is a city with an artist's soul. Home to over 70 artists and sculptors, thousands of visitors each year come to the Loveland to attend the largest sculpture show in the United States.

INNKEEPERS:	Dale & Bev McCue
ADDRESS:	2502 Courtney Drive
	Loveland, CO 80537
TELEPHONE:	(970) 667-3193
E-MAIL:	dmccue31@aol.com
WEBSITE:	www.bbonline.com/co/derbyhill
ROOMS:	2 Rooms; Private baths
CHILDREN:	Children age 12 and older are welcome
ANIMALS:	Not allowed
HANDICAPPED:	Not handicapped accessible
DIETARY NEEDS:	Will accommodate guests' special dietary needs

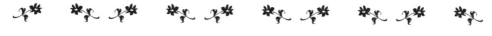

Crispy Potato Quiche

Makes 6 Servings

Hash browns form the unique crust for this breakfast quiche. Some of the preparation can be done in advance. The potato crust can be baked, the sausage (if using) can be browned and the cheeses can be shredded, leaving only the assembling and baking of the quiche for the morning.

1	(24-ounce) package frozen shredded hash browns, thawed
¼	cup (½ stick) butter, melted
1	cup (4 ounces) shredded hot pepper cheese (such as Pepper Jack)
1	cup (4 ounces) shredded Swiss cheese
1	cup (about 6 ounces) diced cooked ham or breakfast sausage
½	cup half & half
2	eggs
¼	teaspoon seasoned salt

Preheat oven to 425°F. Coat a 10-inch quiche dish with non-stick cooking spray. Press thawed hash browns between paper towels to remove excess moisture. Place hash browns into dish and press to form an even, solid crust on the bottom and sides of dish. Brush the crust with melted butter, making certain to brush the top edges. Bake for 25 minutes. Remove from the oven (and cool, cover and refrigerate if preparing ahead). If using sausage, cook until done and drain on paper towels (and cover and refrigerate if preparing ahead).

Lower the oven temperature to 350°F. Layer the sausage or ham over the crust. Next, layer the cheeses. In a small bowl, beat together the half & half, eggs and seasoned salt. Pour the egg mixture over the meat and cheese layers. Bake, uncovered, for 30-40 minutes, or until a knife inserted in the center comes out clean. Leftovers freeze well and can be reheated in the microwave.

> **⚘ Carol's Corner**
>
> *This quiche was a big hit with my "taste-testers." Bev and Dale, innkeepers at Derby Hill Inn, say it's their most frequently requested recipe.*

Wild Horse Inn

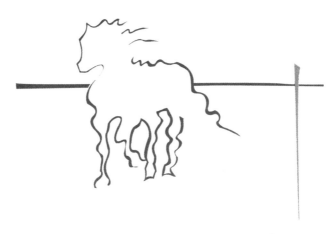

Each of the unique guestrooms of the Wild Horse Inn features vaulted ceilings, private balconies overlooking the forest garden and easy access to the sauna, hot tub and massage room.

"A wonderful place to spend the first two nights of our marriage. Breakfast was amazing, it was peaceful and provided wonderful sleep. We only hope you'll be here in 25 years for our anniversary." — Guest, Wild Horse Inn

INNKEEPERS:	John Cribari & Christine French
ADDRESS:	1536 County Road 83
	Fraser, CO 80442
TELEPHONE:	(970) 726-0456
E-MAIL:	info@wildhorseinncolorado.com
WEBSITE:	www.wildhorseinncolorado.com
ROOMS:	7 Rooms; All with private baths
CHILDREN:	Not allowed
ANIMALS:	Not allowed
HANDICAPPED:	Not handicapped accessible
DIETARY NEEDS:	Will accommodate guests' special dietary needs

Cheddar Shortcakes with Southwestern Hash

Makes 6 Large Servings

The hash contains no meat, so vegetarian guests will be especially pleased with this unique breakfast entrée, which presents beautifully. A side dish of fruit would be the perfect companion.

Shortcakes:

1	cup sour cream
¾	cup ice water
3	cups all-purpose flour
1½	teaspoons baking powder
1	teaspoon baking soda
1½	teaspoons salt
3	tablespoons unsalted butter, chilled and cut into bits
1½	cups (6 ounces) shredded sharp cheddar cheese

Preheat oven to 425°F. Butter or grease a baking sheet. In a small bowl, stir together the sour cream and ice water; set aside.

In a large bowl, sift together the flour, baking powder, baking soda and salt. Add butter to the dry ingredients. Using a pastry blender, cut in the butter until mixture resembles coarse crumbs (you can leave a few larger lumps – these help make the biscuits flakier). Add the cheese and toss. Stir in the thinned sour cream with a fork, until just combined (it should be just barely hanging together).

Turn the dough out onto a lightly floured surface and gather the dough (knead gently a couple times) until it just comes together – don't worry about lumps and bumps. Drop the dough in 6 evenly spaced mounds (about 1 to 1½ inches high) onto the baking sheet.

Recipe continues on page 170…

Cheddar Shortcakes with Southwestern Hash continued...

Bake shortcakes on the middle oven rack for 15-20 minutes, or until light golden brown. Cool shortcakes on a wire rack.

Note: You can make these the night before serving. Cool completely before storing in an airtight container until morning.

Southwestern hash:
½   cup (1 stick) butter
1   large yellow onion, coarsely chopped
6   cloves garlic, minced
1-2 tablespoons chili powder
2   tablespoons dried oregano
6   Yukon Gold potatoes, chopped into 1-inch pieces
1   red bell pepper, chopped
1   (15-ounce) can corn, drained
1   (7-ounce) can diced green chiles
1   bunch fresh cilantro, coarsely chopped
Salt and pepper to taste
Sour cream for garnish

In a very large skillet, melt the butter. Add the onion and garlic; sauté until onions are translucent. Add the chili powder, oregano and potatoes. Cook for 5 minutes. Add the red pepper, corn, diced chiles and most of the cilantro (reserving some cilantro for garnish). Add salt and pepper to taste.

Cover the skillet. Cook until flavors are combined and the potatoes are soft, about 15 minutes. If the hash seems dry, add ¼ cup water and cook until the hash reaches the desired consistency.

To serve: Cut shortcakes in half. Place a bottom half in the middle of each plate. Spoon hash over it, letting some spill out over the plate. Top with the other shortcake half. Garnish with a dollop of sour cream and sprinkle with reserved cilantro.

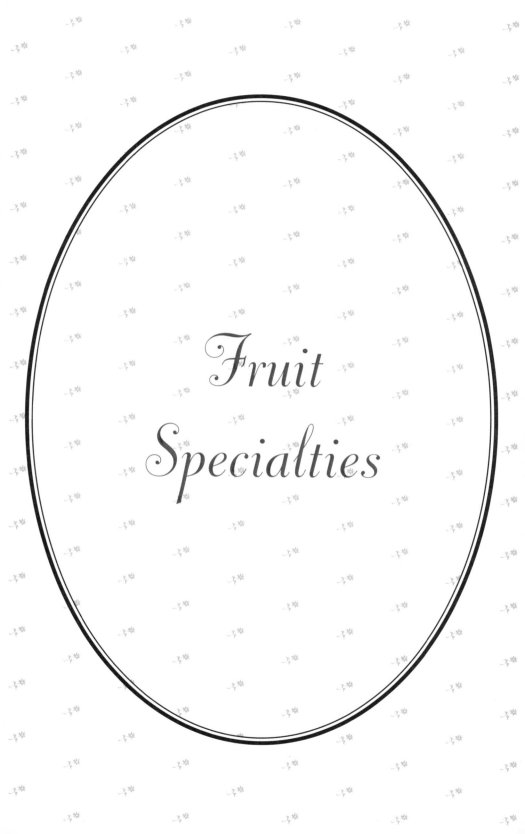

Fruit
Specialties

Silver Wood

S ilver Wood Bed and Breakfast is a contemporary home set in rural Colorado near Divide, where hiking and snowshoeing trails abound. Lake and stream fishing are available for the serious or recreational fisherman.

The Heritage Room offers a special experience for the Silver Wood guest. Select furnishings include a radio from the 1940's, a chest of drawers from the late 1920's and a hand-sewn quilt wall hanging.

INNKEEPERS:	Larry & Bess Oliver
ADDRESS:	463 County Road 512
	Divide, CO 80814
TELEPHONE:	(719) 687-6784; (800) 753-5592
E-MAIL:	innkeeper@silverwoodinn.com
WEBSITE:	www.silverwoodinn.com
ROOMS:	2 Rooms; Both with private baths
CHILDREN:	Welcome
ANIMALS:	Not allowed
HANDICAPPED:	Not handicapped accessible
DIETARY NEEDS:	Will accommodate guests' special dietary needs

Larry's Broiled Grapefruit

Makes 2 Servings (Multiply as Needed)

1   **grapefruit**
2   **tablespoons pure maple syrup**
2   **maraschino cherries**

Preheat broiler. Cut grapefruit in half, crosswise. With a serrated knife, cut out the core, then cut between sections and around the outside edge. Place on foil-lined baking pan (one with a ½-inch edge works best). Fill all empty space in grapefruit halves with maple syrup (about 1 tablespoon per half). Broil about 10 minutes, or until the tops bubble and turn brown (a few black spots are acceptable). Garnish each with a maraschino cherry in the center. Serve warm on a salad plate with a grapefruit spoon.

Frontier's Rest

While sitting in a large, well-worn rocking chair on the Victorian porch of Frontier's Rest Bed and Breakfast Inn, guests listen to a mountain creek and watch the sun set over Pikes Peak. Later they eat homemade cobbler, one of the inn's many complimentary desserts.

This historic home dates back to the turn-of-the-twentieth-century. It has a guest kitchen, delectable breakfasts and a beverage and cookie bar. The inn is located within easy walking distance of local attractions.

INNKEEPERS:	Jeanne Vrobel
ADDRESS:	341 Ruxton Avenue
	Manitou Springs, CO 80829
TELEPHONE:	(719) 685-0588
E-MAIL:	frontierbb@earthlink.net
WEBSITE:	www.colorado-springs-inn.com
ROOMS:	3 Rooms; All with private baths; One cottage
CHILDREN:	Space dependent; Call ahead
ANIMALS:	Not allowed
HANDICAPPED:	Not handicapped accessible
DIETARY NEEDS:	Will accommodate guests' special dietary needs

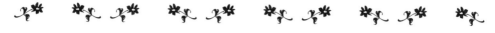

Wake-Up Fruit

Makes 4 Servings

½   cup soft-style cream cheese, regular, low-fat or fat-free variety
½   cup vanilla yogurt
1   tablespoon honey
1   small honeydew melon (or cantaloupe or a combination)
1½ cups fresh raspberries

In a small bowl or in a blender, whip cream cheese, yogurt and honey together until smooth (do not over-whip, or the mixture will become too thin). Slice and peel honeydew melon and arrange on dessert plates. Drizzle cream cheese mixture across the melon wedges. Top with raspberries.

Make-ahead tip: The cream cheese mixture can be made in advance and refrigerated until serving.

Mary Lawrence Inn

The Mary Lawrence Inn is nestled in the scenic Gunnison Valley between the San Juan and Elk Mountains. Built in 1885 by Nathan Weinberger, a local entrepreneur and saloon owner, its subsequent owner, Mary Axtell Lawrence, moved from Illinois to Colorado and finally settled in Gunnison in 1908. Mrs. Lawrence, a widow, served as a teacher and school administrator while operating her home as a boarding house.

This unique Bed and Breakfast was completely renovated in 1989.

INNKEEPERS:	Janette McKinny
ADDRESS:	601 North Taylor
	Gunnison, CO 81230
TELEPHONE:	(970) 641-3343
E-MAIL:	marylinn@gunnison.com
WEBSITE:	www.commerceteam.com/mary.html
ROOMS:	5 Rooms; 2 Suites; All with private baths
CHILDREN:	Welcome
ANIMALS:	Not allowed; Two resident cats
HANDICAPPED:	Not handicapped accessible
DIETARY NEEDS:	Will accommodate guests' special dietary needs

Melon with Peach Salsa

Makes 4 to 8 Servings

In mid-to-late summer, Colorado produces renowned cantaloupes and peaches. This recipe uses both in a unique and colorful way.

3   ripe peaches
2   ripe tomatoes
1   tablespoon lemon juice
3   green onions, sliced
1-2 mild, fresh green chiles (Anaheim), chopped
2   tablespoons fresh cilantro, chopped
¼   cup olive oil
2   tablespoons sherry vinegar
1   tablespoon honey
1-2 ripe Rocky Ford cantaloupes or other melon, cut into wedges
Cilantro sprigs for garnish

Peel peaches and tomatoes; chop coarsely. In a large bowl, combine the peaches and tomatoes with lemon juice. Add green onions, green chiles and cilantro; mix well. In a small bowl, whisk together the oil, vinegar and honey. Pour over fruit and vegetable mixture and stir well. Cover and refrigerate for at least 1 hour before serving.

To serve: Set one wedge of melon upright on a plate. Place salsa on melon. Garnish with cilantro sprig.

Two Sisters Inn

Two Sisters Inn is a gracious bed and breakfast nestled at the base of Pikes Peak. It mixes the charm of the past with the comfort of the present. Built in 1919 by two sisters as the Sunburst boarding house, it showcases an 1896 piano that is tucked into the parlor next to a red velvet fainting couch. An entire wall of cookbooks highlights the library.

"Can I just live here forever?" — Guest, Two Sisters Inn

INNKEEPERS:	Wendy Goldstein & Sharon Smith
ADDRESS:	Ten Otoe Place
	Manitou Springs, CO 80829
TELEPHONE:	(719) 685-9684; (800) 2-SIS-INN
E-MAIL:	twosistersinn@earthlink.net
WEBSITE:	www.twosistersinn.com
ROOMS:	4 Rooms; Private & shared baths; 1 Cottage
CHILDREN:	Children age 10 and older welcome
ANIMALS:	Not allowed
HANDICAPPED:	Not handicapped accessible
DIETARY NEEDS:	Will accommodate guests' special dietary needs

Mango Melon Soup

Makes 6 Servings

"Isn't it amazing how a culinary creation evolves? We needed a fruit course for a breakfast one morning and we searched the refrigerator for what was available. We came up with a ripe mango, some melon and a banana, and quickly whipped up all of these ingredients in a blender. We garnished it with some flowers from our flower and herb gardens and voila – a breakfast soup was born! We are schooled chefs preparing 'creative gourmet' breakfasts. We live to eat!" — Wendy Goldstein and Sharon Smith, Innkeepers at Two Sisters Inn

1	small melon of choice, peeled and cubed
1	ripe banana, peeled
1	mango, peeled and cubed, divided
1	tablespoon fresh lemon juice
1	tablespoon honey

Dash vanilla
6	fresh raspberries for garnish
6	mint leaves for garnish

Place melon cubes in blender and process until smooth. Add banana, ¼ cup mango cubes, lemon juice, honey and vanilla; blend until smooth. Chill mixture for several hours, or overnight. Chill the remaining mango cubes separately.

When ready to serve, divide mango cubes among 6 parfait cups. Stir chilled mixture and pour equally over the fruit. Garnish with raspberries and mint leaves.

Van Horn House

Located in the Roaring Fork Valley, The Van Horn House at Lions Ridge Bed and Breakfast is within minutes of Aspen, Snowmass and Ski Sunlight ski areas. Nearby are the historic towns of Redstone, Marble and Glenwood Springs, home of the world famous hot springs pool.

Each of the four guestrooms has been furnished with antiques, lace curtains, stained glass and just plain charm and coziness!

INNKEEPERS:	John & Susan Laatsch
ADDRESS:	0318 Lions Ridge Road
	Carbondale, CO 81623
TELEPHONE:	(970) 963-3605; (888) 453-0395
E-MAIL:	jlaatsch@aol.com
WEBSITE:	www.vanhornhouse.com
ROOMS:	4 Rooms; Two with private balconies
CHILDREN:	Children age 8 and older are welcome
ANIMALS:	Not allowed; Resident cats
HANDICAPPED:	Not handicapped accessible
DIETARY NEEDS:	Will accommodate guests' special dietary needs

Honey-Poached Pears

Makes 4 Servings

*"The syrup is rich and full of flavor - the honey dominates. This dish is best served at room temperature, although it can be served hot or cold as well." —
Susan Laatsch, The Van Horn House at Lions Ridge*

¾   **cup orange juice**
½   **cup honey**
2   **tablespoons fresh lemon juice**
Pinch of salt
4   **ripe Bartlett pears**
Unsweetened whipping cream, whipped
Cinnamon-sugar (optional)

Combine orange juice, honey, lemon juice and salt in saucepan. Bring to a boil, then reduce heat to a gentle simmer. Peel, halve and core pears; cut into eighths. Add pear slices to honey mixture. Simmer gently for 20 minutes, just until tender. Baste frequently during poaching. Cool in syrup in the pan.

Spoon pear slices and some syrup into attractive serving dishes (stemmed glasses work well). Top with whipped cream and a dash of cinnamon-sugar, if desired.

Plover Inn

The Plover Inn Bed and Breakfast is located on the plains of north-eastern Colorado. James Michener chose this area to symbolize the legendary West in his book *Centennial*. Visitors may recognize the scenic background used in the filming of the television miniseries of the book.

Guests can observe more than 250 species of birds, including the mountain plover, for which The Plover Inn is named. A professional biologist provides birding tours, evening floodlight tours and guide service.

INNKEEPERS:	Joyce Held
ADDRESS:	223 Chatoga Street; PO Box 179
	Grover, CO 80729
TELEPHONE:	(970) 895-2275
E-MAIL:	ploverinn@aol.com
WEBSITE:	Not available
ROOMS:	3 Suites; 2 Rooms; Private and shared baths
CHILDREN:	Welcome
ANIMALS:	Not allowed
HANDICAPPED:	Not handicapped accessible
DIETARY NEEDS:	Will accommodate guests' special dietary needs

Rhubarb Sauce

Makes 1 Quart

"I have an abundance of rhubarb plants, so in the spring and summer, rhubarb is always on the menu. I use rhubarb in a lot of standard recipes such as muffins, coffee cakes, breads and sauces. This rhubarb sauce is a favorite over pancakes." — *Joyce Held, Plover Inn*

4	cups chopped rhubarb
2	cups sugar
¼	cup water
1	(8-ounce) package raspberry or strawberry Jell-O
1	teaspoon cinnamon

Combine rhubarb, sugar and water in saucepan and let sit for at least 30 minutes, stirring occasionally. Bring to a boil, reduce heat to low and simmer – 10 minutes for firm rhubarb, or 20-30 minutes for softer rhubarb. Add Jell-O and cinnamon. Stir to dissolve. Serve warm over pancakes, waffles or French toast.

Note: This recipe can be cut in half using a 3-ounce package of gelatin.

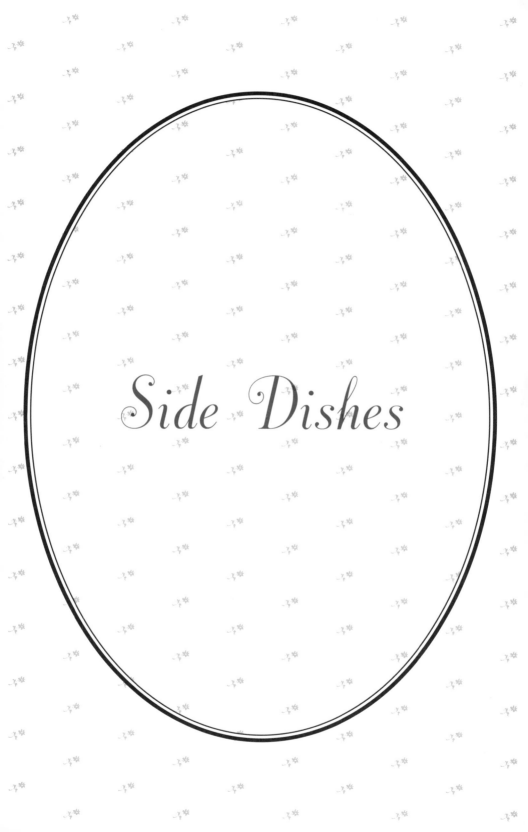

Side Dishes

Apple Orchard Inn

Owners John and Celeste Gardiner moved back to the United States in 1995 after having lived in Europe for six years. A few months later, they purchased the Apple Orchard Inn Bed and Breakfast.

While living in Europe, Celeste took a course in general cuisine as well as pastry making at the Ritz-Escoffier Ecole de Gastronomie Française in Paris, France. She also studied "one-on-one" with Judy Witts Francini in Florence, Italy, where she learned Northern Italian cooking.

INNKEEPERS:	John & Celeste Gardiner
ADDRESS:	7758 County Road 203
	Durango, CO 81301
TELEPHONE:	(970) 247-0751; (800) 426-0751
E-MAIL:	info@appleorchardinn.com
WEBSITE:	www.appleorchardinn.com
ROOMS:	4 Rooms; 6 Cottages; All with private baths
CHILDREN:	Welcome
ANIMALS:	Not allowed; Resident pets
HANDICAPPED:	Limited Access
DIETARY NEEDS:	Will accommodate guests' special dietary needs

Rosemary Roasted Potatoes

Makes 6 Servings

These oven-roasted potatoes are delicious for breakfast or for dinner with meat.

2   pounds new potatoes, cut into 1-inch cubes
3   tablespoons olive oil
2   tablespoons chopped fresh rosemary leaves
2   teaspoons dried thyme
1   teaspoon freshly ground black pepper
1   teaspoon coarsely ground salt

Preheat oven to 350°F. Place potatoes in a large mixing bowl. Add olive oil, herbs and spices and mix thoroughly (or shake to coat in a sealed zip-seal bag). Coat a shallow roasting pan with non-stick cooking spray. Spread potatoes in a single layer in the pan. Bake for about 45 minutes, stirring every 15 minutes or so, until potatoes are browned on the outside and tender in the center.

Serving suggestion: After roasting the potatoes, add sautéed diced onion and green pepper. Place potato mixture in individual serving dishes and top with eggs (either fried, scrambled or poached) and sprinkle with cheddar cheese. Bake for a few minutes to melt cheese. Garnish with chopped chives and serve.

Abriendo Inn

S erved individually in the sunny breakfast room or on one of the picturesque porches, the typical morning meal at the Abriendo Inn Bed and Breakfast is hearty, tasty and for anyone who enjoys the pleasure and indulgence of a full breakfast. Breakfast baskets also are available for those who wish to dine in their rooms.

"The breakfast was, by itself, worth the stay." — Guest, Abriendo Inn

INNKEEPERS:	Kerrelyn Trent
ADDRESS:	300 West Abriendo Avenue
	Pueblo, CO 81004
TELEPHONE:	(719) 544-2703
E-MAIL:	info@abriendoinn.com
WEBSITE:	www.abriendoinn.com
ROOMS:	10 Rooms; All with private baths
CHILDREN:	Children age 7 and older are welcome
ANIMALS:	Not allowed
HANDICAPPED:	Not handicapped accessible
DIETARY NEEDS:	Will accommodate guests' special dietary needs

Grilled Lime Potatoes

Makes 6 Servings

"I don't think we have ever served these grilled lime potatoes without someone raving about them. This recipe is one of several developed for our 'Barbeque Breakfasts' that we serve on Saturday mornings from the weekend after Labor Day to the last Saturday in October." — Kerrelyn Trent, Abriendo Inn

4	large potatoes, peeled and cut into 1-inch cubes
¼	cup (½ stick) butter, melted
2	limes, juiced (about 2-3 tablespoons lime juice)
1-2	green onions, chopped
1	teaspoon salt
¼	teaspoon pepper

Place the cubed potatoes in a large pot. Add enough water to cover and bring to a boil. Reduce heat to low and cover the pot. Simmer 10-15 minutes, or until fork-tender. Drain well. Refrigerate until well chilled.

In a large bowl, combine the melted butter, lime juice, chopped green onion, salt and pepper. Add the chilled potatoes and mix gently to combine. The potatoes are now ready to grill.

Alternate method: The cooked and drained potatoes can be combined with the butter/lime mixture while the potatoes are still warm. Completely chill the potatoes before grilling.

Preheat grill. Arrange potatoes on an oiled grill screen (or in an oiled grill basket) and place on the grill rack. Grill, turning the potatoes two or three times with a spatula, until lightly browned, about 10-15 minutes.

> *Carol's Corner*
> *Abriendo Inn says the lime-marinated potatoes can be grilled in advance and refrigerated; the flavor intensifies. Reheat the potatoes on a baking sheet in the oven before serving. This is a particularly helpful tip when feeding a large group.*

Frontier's Rest

Tucked away at the back of Frontier's Rest Bed and Breakfast is the Belle Room. The window opens to a 100-year-old, stone terraced wall and a naturally forested hillside. Guests relax on a seven-foot Renaissance Revival queen-size bed. A bath is attached, featuring an oval tub and shower combination and an authentic pedestal sink.

"To sleep in the treetops at the foot of the Rockies. Sound like a dream? It happens here every night." — Owner, Jeanne Vrobel

INNKEEPERS:	Jeanne Vrobel
ADDRESS:	341 Ruxton Avenue
	Manitou Springs, CO 80829
TELEPHONE:	(719) 685-0588
E-MAIL:	frontierbb@earthlink.net
WEBSITE:	www.colorado-springs-inn.com
ROOMS:	3 Rooms; All with private baths; One cottage
CHILDREN:	Space dependent; Call ahead
ANIMALS:	Not allowed
HANDICAPPED:	Not handicapped accessible
DIETARY NEEDS:	Will accommodate guests' special dietary needs

Frontier Potatoes

Makes 2 Servings

Pungent and savory, the whole cumin seeds give these potatoes a very distinctive flavor ... a dish that would be welcome at breakfast, brunch or dinner.

6-8   red potatoes, unpeeled
3   slices bacon, chopped
½   red or orange bell pepper, sliced into thin strips
2   tablespoons butter
1   teaspoon whole cumin seeds

Boil potatoes in a saucepan with water until tender. Drain potatoes when done and cut into chunky slices.

Melt butter in a large skillet. Add bacon and red pepper and sauté until bell pepper is crisp-tender. Add potatoes and cumin seeds. Cook until potatoes are browned.

The Gable House

The Gable House Bed and Breakfast is located on a picturesque, tree-lined street in the heart of historic Durango. Rooms are intimate and elegantly furnished with antiques, and each has a private entrance. Queen, double and single beds are available, as well as extra space if needed.

The Gable House is conveniently located five blocks from the Durango and Silverton Narrow Gauge Railroad Station, and is just a few blocks from downtown Durango's delightful shops and restaurants.

INNKEEPERS:	Heather Bryson
ADDRESS:	805 East Fifth Avenue
	Durango, CO 81301
TELEPHONE:	(970) 247-4982
E-MAIL:	ghbb@frontier.net
WEBSITE:	www.creativelinks.com/gablehouse
ROOMS:	3 Rooms; All with private baths
CHILDREN:	Children age 10 and older are welcome
ANIMALS:	Not allowed
HANDICAPPED:	Not handicapped accessible
DIETARY NEEDS:	Will accommodate guests' special dietary needs

Heather's Pappas

Makes 4 Servings

4   large potatoes, parboiled (partially cooked)
4   tablespoons butter
4   tablespoons flour
4   cups chicken broth
2   tablespoons dried, mild green chile powder (see *Carol's Corner*)
¾   cup heavy cream
Salt and pepper to taste
2   tablespoons Canola oil
4   large eggs
1   cup (4 ounces) shredded cheddar cheese
Chopped parsley for garnish
Flour tortillas for accompaniment

Cook potatoes the night before and refrigerate. In the morning, make a roux: In a saucepan over medium heat, melt butter. Stir in flour and cook, stirring constantly, until mixture is smooth and bubbly. Pour in chicken broth and green chile powder. While stirring, bring to a boil. It will thicken somewhat, but will still have a soup-like consistency. Blend in heavy cream. Add salt and pepper to taste.

Sauté potatoes in canola oil until brown. Fry or poach eggs. To assemble: Place ¼ of potatoes in a soup bowl, cover with ¼ of green chile sauce. Sprinkle with cheddar cheese and place an egg on top. Garnish with chopped parsley and serve with warm tortillas on the side.

Tip: The sauce can be prepared in advance and frozen.

> *Carol's Corner*
> *Heather, at the Gable House, buys green chile powder at roadside stands on the road between Albuquerque and her home in Durango. The chile powder can be ordered from Hatch Chile Express (505) 267-3226 or www.hatch-chile.com).*

Evans House

Located in the heart of Breckenridge, the Evans House Bed and Breakfast offers a fully restored 1886 Victorian home. Each room celebrates different heroes of the local area.

"We liked nothing better than coming 'home' to the gas fireplace, slipping on comfy robes and then into the hot tub to relax our sore muscles. We really enjoyed Father Dyer's writings. What a wonderful way to spend our first anniversary. Next year, we'll bring the baby."— Guest, Evans House

INNKEEPERS:	Peter & Georgette Contos
ADDRESS:	102 South French Street
	Breckenridge, CO 80424
TELEPHONE:	(970) 453-5509
E-MAIL:	evans15@mindspring.com
WEBSITE:	www.coloradoevanshouse.com
ROOMS:	6 Rooms; 2 Suites; All with private baths
CHILDREN:	Welcome
ANIMALS:	Not allowed
HANDICAPPED:	Limited accessibility
DIETARY NEEDS:	Will accommodate guests' special dietary needs

Greek Salad

Makes 8 Servings

Enjoy this flavorful salad with a loaf of hot Italian bread.

1	head Romaine lettuce, torn into pieces
1	cucumber, sliced
1	green pepper, sliced
3	green onions, chopped
1	tomato, cut into chunks
½	cup olive oil
¼	cup red wine or balsamic vinegar
1½	teaspoons chopped fresh oregano
½	teaspoon chopped fresh dill
¼	cup crumbled feta cheese
12	pitted kalamata olives

On a serving platter or in a large bowl, combine the lettuce with the cucumber, green pepper, green onions and tomato.

In a small bowl, whisk together the olive oil, wine vinegar, oregano and dill. Drizzle the dressing over the salad. Sprinkle with feta cheese and top with olives.

Abriendo Inn

S ince the Abriendo Inn Bed and Breakfast opened in 1989, Christmas has been a special time. Countless hours are spent each season bringing the glow and spirit of Christmas to the entire inn. Each guestroom has its own uniquely decorated Christmas tree. Holiday garlands of evergreen and ribbon adorn the French doors, fireplace and windows throughout the common areas of the inn.

The jewel of the décor is the towering evergreen tree in the parlor.

INNKEEPERS:	Kerrelyn Trent
ADDRESS:	300 West Abriendo Avenue
	Pueblo, CO 81004
TELEPHONE:	(719) 544-2703
E-MAIL:	info@abriendoinn.com
WEBSITE:	www.abriendoinn.com
ROOMS:	10 Rooms; All with private baths
CHILDREN:	Children age 7 and older are welcome
ANIMALS:	Not allowed
HANDICAPPED:	Not handicapped accessible
DIETARY NEEDS:	Will accommodate guests' special dietary needs

Orange & Black Bean Salsa

Makes 3¼ Cups

Serve this brilliant-colored salsa with grilled chicken, pork tenderloin, swordfish or Mexican dishes. It is best the day it is prepared, but do make it 1-2 hours in advance to allow the flavors to combine.

1   (15-ounce) can mandarin oranges
1   (15-ounce) can black beans
1   plum tomato, chopped
1   large (or 2 small) green onions, chopped
⅓   cup chopped cilantro (more or less to taste)
1   tablespoon olive oil
Pinch of cayenne pepper, or more to taste
1¼   teaspoon salt

Drain mandarin oranges and place in a large bowl. Using a colander or strainer, rinse the black beans with water and drain well. Add the tomatoes, green onions and cilantro to the mandarin oranges, along with the drained black beans. Stir in the olive oil, cayenne pepper and salt. Mix well. Refrigerate for 1-2 hours before serving.

Dinner Entrées

Conejos Ranch

For over 100 years, the Conejos Ranch has been the traveler's choice in south-central Colorado. Noted for its Western hospitality and charm, guests enjoy excellent accommodations and breathtaking scenery.

The Conejos River Ranch is nestled in the Rio Grande National Forest with a mile of Conejos River frontage, and has been featured in *America's Wonderful Little Hotels and Inns.*

INNKEEPERS:	Ms. Shorty Fry
ADDRESS:	25390 Highway 17
	Antonito, CO 81120
TELEPHONE:	(719) 376-2464
E-MAIL:	info@conejosranch.com
WEBSITE:	www.conejosranch.com.com
ROOMS:	8 Rooms; All with private baths; 6 Log Cabins
CHILDREN:	Welcome
ANIMALS:	Welcome
HANDICAPPED:	Handicapped accessible
DIETARY NEEDS:	Will accommodate guests' special dietary needs

Conejos Ranch Cornish Game Hens

Makes 2 Servings

Remember to plan ahead for this recipe. Rock Cornish game hens usually come frozen, so allow thawing time in the refrigerator or microwave. Remove giblet package from thawed hen before cooking.

2	Rock Cornish game hens

Salt
Pepper
Granulated garlic

1-2	apples, chopped
½	cup (1 stick) butter
1	medium onion, diced
¼	cup cream sherry

Wash hens and pat dry. Rub inside of the hens with salt, pepper and granulated garlic. Stuff the apples inside the hens (if the hens are small, only 1 apple may be needed). Place hens breast side up on a rack in a roasting pan.

Preheat oven to 350°F. Melt the butter in a skillet and sauté the onions with the cream sherry until the onions are translucent. Put this mixture on top of the hens. Cover with foil or a lid. Bake for 30-40 minutes. Remove the foil and bake for 30 minutes more, or until golden brown.

Outpost Inn

For many years, Barbara Parker had been enjoying her visits to the Rocky Mountains. When she realized this experience was something she wanted to have on a permanent basis, she moved from New Jersey to Colorado. After a two-year search, she picked the Outpost Bed and Breakfast and Winter Park as her new residence.

"Come share the experience. Share the Rocky Mountains with us!" — Owner, Barbara Parker

INNKEEPERS:	Barbara Parker
ADDRESS:	PO Box 41
	Winter Park, CO 80482
TELEPHONE:	(970) 726-5346; (800) 430-4538
E-MAIL:	barbarajane@winterparkweb.com
WEBSITE:	www.winterpark-inn.com
ROOMS:	7 Rooms; All with private baths
CHILDREN:	Welcome
ANIMALS:	Not allowed; Resident pets
HANDICAPPED:	Not handicapped accessible
DIETARY NEEDS:	Will accommodate guests' special dietary needs

Cilantro Chicken

Makes 6 Servings

"It has become my tradition to serve this low-fat dish to celebrate Cinco de Mayo." — *Barbara Parker, Outpost Inn*

1	pound boneless, skinless chicken breasts
	Cajun spice (hot)
	Olive oil
1	large Spanish onion, coarsely chopped
1	large green bell pepper, coarsely chopped
8	Roma tomatoes, chopped
1	(16-ounce) jar mild picante sauce
¼	cup chopped cilantro

Cut chicken breasts into chunks and season with Cajun spice to taste. Heat olive oil in skillet and brown chicken. Add onions and peppers; sauté until onions are translucent. Add tomatoes; cover and simmer for 15 minutes. Add picante sauce and cilantro. Cover and simmer slowly for 1 hour, or until chicken is very tender. Serve with yellow rice and black beans.

Make-ahead tip: This dish can be prepared in advance and frozen.

Apple Orchard Inn

Owners John and Celeste Gardiner lived in Europe for six years before returning to the United States in 1995. While in Belgium, Celeste prepared the dessert for the restaurant in the American Women's Club of Brussels. She later taught cooking classes for the American women.

Each of the guestrooms and cottages is uniquely trimmed with exquisite hardwoods and features elegant furnishings.

INNKEEPERS:	John & Celeste Gardiner
ADDRESS:	7758 County Road 203
	Durango, CO 81301
TELEPHONE:	(970) 247-0751; (800) 426-0751
E-MAIL:	info@appleorchardinn.com
WEBSITE:	www.appleorchardinn.com
ROOMS:	4 Rooms; All with private baths; 6 Cottages
CHILDREN:	Welcome
ANIMALS:	Not allowed; Resident pets
HANDICAPPED:	Limited Access
DIETARY NEEDS:	Will accommodate guests' special dietary needs

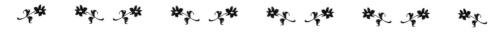

Chicken Breasts on a Bed of Wild Mushrooms

Makes 4 Servings

"We have had wonderful success with our dinners. Our guests really seem to enjoy the luxury of having dinner at the inn and then being able to retire to their rooms." — *John and Celeste Gardiner, Apple Orchard Inn*

2	cups chicken broth
2	ounces dried mushrooms (cèpes, morels, trompettes des mortes or a combination), thoroughly rinsed and drained
1	pound fresh white mushrooms
6	tablespoons (¾ stick) unsalted butter
4	boneless, skinless chicken breasts, halved
½	cup finely chopped shallots

Salt and freshly ground black pepper to taste

1	cup white Port wine
1	cup heavy cream

Bring the broth to a boil in a small saucepan. Pour it over the dried mushrooms in a small bowl. Let stand for at least 2 hours. Meanwhile, trim stems from white mushrooms and thinly slice.

Melt butter in skillet. Add chicken and brown lightly. Cover and simmer on low heat for about 15 minutes, turning after 7 minutes. Remove chicken from pan; pour a little of melted butter over them and keep warm while preparing the sauce.

Pour off all but about 2 tablespoons of fat and add the shallots. Sauté gently for about 5 minutes without browning. Drain and coarsely chop the dried mushrooms, reserving the liquid. Add the dried mushrooms and the sliced white mushrooms to skillet and simmer for 10 minutes, stirring occasionally. Season with salt and pepper. Add the reserved mushroom soaking liquid and wine to skillet and simmer for 5 minutes, or until slightly thickened. Add the cream and simmer until the sauce is thick enough to coat a spoon. Place chicken breasts on top of the mushroom sauce, cover and simmer for 5 minutes before serving.

Ellen's

The appeal of Ellen's Bed and Breakfast is the homey atmosphere and good conversation. The one guestroom has a four-poster bed and a private bath with an old-fashioned, bright green, claw-footed bathtub. An additional small room with bunk beds accommodates two children.

Ellen sets her breakfast table with crystal and china and serves Eggs Benedict with asparagus, a three-cheese Santa Fe quiche or pecan waffles.

INNKEEPERS:	Baldwin & Ellen Ranson
ADDRESS:	700 Kimbark Street
	Longmont, CO 80501
TELEPHONE:	(303) 776-1676
E-MAIL:	ellen@ellensbandb.com
WEBSITE:	www.ellensbandb.com
ROOMS:	2 Rooms; Private baths
CHILDREN:	Welcome
ANIMALS:	Welcome; Resident pets
HANDICAPPED:	Not handicapped accessible
DIETARY NEEDS:	Will accommodate guests' special dietary needs

Sweet & Sauerkraut Ribs

Makes 3 to 4 Servings

"Serve this HOT with homemade mashed potatoes. Good stuff for a winter day! Brown sugar is the key. Freezes well." — Ellen Ranson, Ellen's B&B

1	large (32-ounce) can or bag good brand sauerkraut
1	cup water
½	cup packed brown sugar (or more to your taste)
6-7	country style pork ribs (gotta be country style!)
½	red apple, unpeeled and finely chopped

Preheat oven to 325°F. Coat a 13x9-inch baking dish with non-stick cooking spray. Put sauerkraut in the dish. Mix in about 1 cup of water and the brown sugar. Lay ribs on top. Cover tightly with foil.

Bake s-l-o-w-l-y all afternoon (about 4 hours). Then drain off some of the fatty liquid. Stir in red apple and bake, uncovered, for another 30 minutes.

> *Carol's Corner*
> *I am very fond of sauerkraut so this is one of my favorites! Try putting it in a crockpot (along with some onion slices and omitting the apple, for variety) before you go to work in the morning. You'll love having dinner ready when you arrive home.*

Wyman Hotel and Inn

L ocated at an elevation of 9,318 feet, the Wyman Hotel and Inn offers the privacy of a hotel with the ambiance of a bed and breakfast inn. This totally renovated, historic 1902 red-sandstone corner building has 24-inch thick walls, cathedral ceilings and arched windows.

Romantic amenities include breakfast in bed, beautiful floral bouquets, romantic picnic lunches and champagne or wine and cheese baskets.

INNKEEPERS:	Lorraine & Tom Lewis
ADDRESS:	1371 Greene Street
	Silverton, CO 81433
TELEPHONE:	(970) 387-5372; (800) 609-7845
E-MAIL:	thewyman@frontier.net
WEBSITE:	www.thewyman.com
ROOMS:	18 Rooms; All with private baths
CHILDREN:	Well-behaved children are welcome
ANIMALS:	Welcome in certain rooms
HANDICAPPED:	Is handicapped accessible
DIETARY NEEDS:	Will accommodate guests' special dietary needs

Curried Pork Saté

Makes 4 Servings

Saté [sah-TAY], sometimes spelled satay, *is often served in small portions as an appetizer, but here it is presented as a main dish. It's a beautiful display to see these colorful shish kabobs served on a bed of wild rice and steamed mushrooms.*

¼   cup soy sauce
¼   cup extra virgin olive oil
¼   cup dry red wine
1   tablespoon fresh lime juice
1   tablespoon dark brown sugar
1   tablespoon curry powder
1   teaspoon cumin powder
1½ teaspoons red pepper flakes
2   pounds lean boneless pork, cut into strips (¼-inch thick, 1-inch wide, 8-inch long)
4   ounces grape tomatoes
4   ounces white pearl onions, ends cut off, but skins left on

In a large bowl (or zipper-seal plastic bag), combine the soy sauce, olive oil, wine, lime juice, brown sugar, curry powder, cumin and red pepper flakes. Mix well. Add the pork and mix to thoroughly coat the meat. Refrigerate for at least 3 hours, stirring occasionally to keep the meat coated.

Remove the meat from marinade and place the strips on a wire rack to let excess marinade drip off. Reserve the marinade. Weave pork strips (back and forth, like sewing) on long skewers, alternating with tomatoes and onions. Cook until done on a preheated, well-oiled grill for about 15 minutes, turning frequently and basting with reserved marinade for the first 5 minutes of the cooking time. Serve with wild rice and sautéed mushrooms.

> *Carol's Corner*
> *A grape tomato is a miniature, sweet variety of tomato that grows in clusters like grapes. If grape tomatoes are not available, cherry tomatoes may be substituted.*

Evans House

Located within walking distance of numerous shops and restaurants, the Evans House Bed and Breakfast is a traditional bed and breakfast, listed in the National Historic Register.

Summer activities include hiking, biking, jeep tours, horseback rides, historical mining tours and music festivals. Winter activities include downhill and cross-country skiing, ice skating, snowmobiling, sleigh rides and snowshoeing.

INNKEEPERS:	Peter & Georgette Contos
ADDRESS:	102 South French Street
	Breckenridge, CO 80424
TELEPHONE:	(970) 453-5509
E-MAIL:	evans15@mindspring.com
WEBSITE:	www.coloradoevanshouse.com
ROOMS:	6 Rooms; 2 Suites; All with private baths
CHILDREN:	Welcome
ANIMALS:	Not allowed
HANDICAPPED:	Limited accessibility
DIETARY NEEDS:	Will accommodate guests' special dietary needs

Shish Kabobs with Tzatziki Sauce

Makes 8 Servings

Plan ahead: The meat needs to marinate overnight, and the tzatziki sauce should be made and chilled a day in advance for full flavor development. The sauce is a great accompaniment to meats, or it can be used as a dip for pita bread or fresh vegetables. It's also a great dressing for gyro or souvlaki sandwiches.

1   cup olive oil
2   lemons, juiced
1   tablespoon chopped fresh oregano
1   teaspoon garlic salt
1   pork tenderloin, about 2½ pounds
Tzatziki sauce (recipe below)

In a large baking dish, whisk together the olive oil, lemon juice, oregano and garlic salt to make a marinade. Cut the pork into cubes and thread them onto wooden sticks or metal skewers. Marinate the meat overnight in the marinade, turning frequently.

Cook the kabobs over a hot, well-oiled grill until done, about 15 minutes, turning the skewers frequently for even cooking. Serve with tzatziki sauce.

Tzatziki sauce:
1   cucumber, peeled
1   (16-ounce) container plain yogurt
4   cloves garlic
1   tablespoon olive oil
1   tablespoon white vinegar

Cut cucumber in half lengthwise. Using a spoon, scrape out the seeds. Chop the cucumber into small cubes. Place the cubes in a strainer and drain for about 20 minutes. With a paper towel, blot as much excess liquid as possible. In a food processor or blender, combine the yogurt, garlic, olive oil and vinegar. Purée until smooth. Place the yogurt mixture into a bowl; stir in the drained cucumber. Refrigerate overnight. Makes 2½ to 3 cups.

B uilt in the mid-1960's, the Kelly Place Bed and Breakfast Lodge is an adobe-style building with courtyards. It is located just west of Cortez in McElmo Canyon, where over 25 Anasazi sites have been documented.

A full-time archaeologist teaches archaeology classes and oversees the excavation and restoration of the sites. The Lodge borders 6,000 acres of Anasazi sites and hiking trails.

INNKEEPERS:	Kristie Carriker
ADDRESS:	14663 County Road G
	Cortez, CO 81321
TELEPHONE:	(970) 565-3125; (800) 745-4885
E-MAIL:	kellypl@fone.net
WEBSITE:	www.kellyplace.com
ROOMS:	8 Rooms; All with private baths
CHILDREN:	No charge for children age 6 and under
ANIMALS:	Not allowed; Resident pet
HANDICAPPED:	Not handicapped accessible
DIETARY NEEDS:	Will accommodate guests' special dietary needs

Kelly Place Beef & Beans

Makes 4 Servings

2	cups dry pinto beans
4	cups water
2	pounds pot roast
1	large onion, chopped
1	tablespoon salt
1	cup ketchup
½	cup dark molasses
2	tablespoons yellow mustard
1	teaspoon liquid smoke
5-6	pieces crystallized ginger

Soak the beans overnight in the water in a large soup pot. The next morning, add the pot roast, onion and salt to the beans and their soaking liquid. Cook over medium-low heat until the meat is done, adding more water as needed, but not so much as to make a great deal of broth.

Remove the roast; debone and strip the beef into bite-size pieces. Return the beef to the beans and add remaining ingredients. Simmer at least 4 hours, the longer the better. And, as with most bean dishes ... it's better the next day!

Carol's Corner

Want to eliminate the stress of cooking and kitchen clean-up when you are entertaining? Make this recipe a day in advance, or even several days or weeks in advance and freeze it. It can also be made in a crockpot.

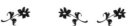

Casa de Paz

The Casa de Paz Bed and Breakfast is located in the beautiful, scenic southwestern area of the Beulah Valley, 25 miles west of Pueblo. A six acre back yard is bordered by locust and pine trees. One particular ponderosa pine stands 150 feet tall and is more than 200 years old.

The Sanctuary of St. Jude chapel is adjacent to the living room and can seat 45 people.

INNKEEPERS:	Harry & Ann Middelkamp
ADDRESS:	8733 Pine Drive
	Beulah, CO 81023
TELEPHONE:	(719) 485-3201
E-MAIL:	Not available
WEBSITE:	www.puebloonline.com/beulah
ROOMS:	4 Rooms; All with private baths
CHILDREN:	Welcome
ANIMALS:	Welcome
HANDICAPPED:	Is handicapped accessible
DIETARY NEEDS:	Will accommodate guests' special dietary needs

Kibbe

Makes 8 to 10 Servings

"We owe these good dishes – that our guests love – to Nabeha Fidel Koury, a wonderful cook and a wonderful lady. I have noticed that our friends that have an Egyptian background make Kibbe as below, but add cinnamon and allspice as well." — *Ann Middelkamp, Casa de Paz*

2½ pounds finely ground lamb (or lean hamburger)
1 large onion, grated
¼ cup chopped mint (or to taste)
1 cup cracked wheat or bulgur (soaked for 10 minutes in 2 cups water)

Combine the meat, onion, mint and wheat (or bulgur) in a large bowl. Put half of this mixture in the bottom of an 8x12-inch baking pan.

Stuffing mix (middle layer):
1 pound finely ground lamb (or lean hamburger)
1 small onion, chopped finely
¼ cup piñon nuts, or more to your taste
½ cup (1 stick) butter (not margarine), sliced

Preheat oven to 350°F. In a large skillet, cook the lamb, onion and piñon nuts together, until lamb is nearly done. Cool and put on top of raw mixture in baking pan. Cover stuffing with remaining lamb/mint mixture. Score meat mixture into diamond shapes. Lay sliced butter on top. Bake for 1 hour, or until butter disappears into meat. Serve with Lebanese salad.

Lebanese salad:
½ cup salad vinegar or lemon juice
½ cup olive oil
2 cloves garlic, minced
Mint to taste

Combine ingredients by shaking in a jar. Refrigerate until ready to use. Just before serving, pour dressing over chopped iceberg or romaine lettuce, and sliced onion, cucumbers and tomatoes; toss well.

Wyman Hotel & Inn

Built in 1902, the Wyman Hotel & Inn was originally designed as a ballroom and banquet hall. On September 19, 2002, the Inn commemorated its 100th anniversary with a Victorian party.

"The attention to detail and comfort was great. I will be telling all my friends about the Wyman. They helped make our anniversary wonderful." — Guest, Wyman Hotel & Inn

INNKEEPERS:	Lorraine & Tom Lewis
ADDRESS:	1371 Greene Street
	Silverton, CO 81433
TELEPHONE:	(970) 387-5372; (800) 609-7845
E-MAIL:	thewyman@frontier.net
WEBSITE:	www.thewyman.com
ROOMS:	18 Rooms; All with private baths
CHILDREN:	Well-behaved children are welcome
ANIMALS:	Welcome in certain rooms
HANDICAPPED:	Is handicapped accessible
DIETARY NEEDS:	Will accommodate guests' special dietary needs

Bedouin Lamb

Makes 3 to 4 Servings

Bedouin [bed-oo-in] is the name of various tribes of nomadic Arabian desert dwellers. This lamb shish kabob recipe is a Middle Eastern-inspired dish. If desired, baby carrots, zucchini, onions, bell peppers or other vegetables can be added to the skewers before grilling.

¼   cup soy sauce
¼   cup extra virgin olive oil
¼   cup dry red wine
2   tablespoons fresh lime juice
3   tablespoons chopped fresh rosemary
1   teaspoon dark brown sugar
1½   pounds lean boneless lamb, cut into 1-inch cubes
Cooked rice for serving
Slivered almonds for garnish
Chopped walnuts for garnish

In a large bowl (or zipper-seal plastic bag), combine all of the ingredients, except the lamb. Mix well. Add the lamb and mix to coat. Refrigerate for at least 6-8 hours, stirring occasionally to keep the meat coated.

Remove the lamb from the marinade, reserving the marinade for basting the meat while grilling. Thread the lamb on long metal skewers and cook on a hot, well-oiled grill for about 15 minutes, turning frequently and basting with the marinade during the first 5 minutes of cooking time. Present the grilled shish kabobs on a platter over a bed of rice, sprinkled with almonds and walnuts.

Carol's Corner

Tom Lewis, an ex-engineer, now an innkeeper (with his wife Lorraine) and chef extraordinaire, spent considerable time working in the Middle East many years ago. This lamb recipe is his interpretation of a similar dish he used to eat while living and traveling in the Arabian desert.

River Run Inn

S et amidst the majestic Rocky Mountains and the graceful Arkansas River, the River Run Inn is a turn-of-the-twentieth-century country home. All bedrooms feature antique poster beds, comfortable mattresses and most have mountain views. For larger groups, the third floor offers a dormitory with 13 beds, a large bath, table and chairs.

This cozy bed and breakfast inn is ideal for reunions, group stays, weddings and other special events.

INNKEEPERS:	Virginia Nemmers
ADDRESS:	8495 County Road 160
	Salida, CO 81201
TELEPHONE:	(719) 539-3818
E-MAIL:	riverrun@amigo.net
WEBSITE:	www.riverruninn.com
ROOMS:	8 Rooms; All with private baths
CHILDREN:	Children age 10 and older are welcome
ANIMALS:	Not allowed; Resident dog
HANDICAPPED:	Not handicapped accessible
DIETARY NEEDS:	Will accommodate guests' special dietary needs

Virginia's Baked Trout

Number of Servings Depends on Number and Size of Fish

Here's an easy recipe for your fresh catch!

Whole trout, deboned
Butter, melted
Herbs of choice, chopped (dill, herbes de Provence, thyme, basil, etc.)
Lemon, thinly sliced

Rinse trout thoroughly with water; pat dry inside and out. Drizzle inside of trout with melted butter. Sprinkle with herbs and lay thin slices of lemon along the inside of the fish. Drizzle outside of fish with more melted butter and lay a few lemon slices on top. Securely wrap fish with foil and place on a large baking sheet. Bake about 20 minutes for larger fish, less time for smaller fish.

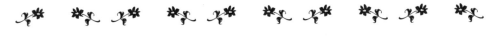

Garden House

Located in Palisade, the Peach Capital of Colorado, the Garden House Bed and Breakfast is a spacious tri-level country home that boasts beautiful oak floors, large bay windows and high-beamed ceilings. The French country décor provides a feeling of casual elegance.

The scrumptious gourmet country breakfast features entrées such as Grand Mesa quiche, ranch eggs tarragon and baked caramel French toast.

INNKEEPERS:	Bill & Joyce Haas
ADDRESS:	3587 G Road
	Palisade, CO 81526
TELEPHONE:	(970) 464-4686; (800) 305-4686
E-MAIL:	bjgardenhouse@cs.com
WEBSITE:	www.colorado-bnb.com/gardnhse
ROOMS:	2 Rooms; 2 Suites; All with private baths
CHILDREN:	Children age 12 and older are welcome
ANIMALS:	Not allowed; Resident dog & outside cat
HANDICAPPED:	Not handicapped accessible
DIETARY NEEDS:	Will accommodate guests' special dietary needs

Seafood Casserole

Makes 6 Large Servings

¼ cup (½ stick) butter
⅓ cup chopped onion
¼ cup all-purpose flour
1 cup milk
1 cup heavy cream or half & half
½ teaspoon salt
½ teaspoon pepper
Pinch of red pepper
1 teaspoon Old Bay seafood seasoning, or more to taste
1 tablespoon chopped dried parsley
1 (8-ounce) can sliced water chestnuts, drained
1 (4-ounce) jar diced pimentos
2 tablespoons fresh lemon juice
2 (6-ounce) cans white crab meat (1 cup crab meat)
1 pound cooked and peeled shrimp
3 cups cooked rice
1 cup shredded Havarti or Swiss cheese
¾ cup shredded Parmesan cheese

Preheat oven to 350°F. Coat an 8x8-inch square baking dish with nonstick cooking spray. In a large skillet, melt the butter and sauté the onions until translucent. Blend in the flour. Add milk and cream; cook and stir until thickened and bubbly. Remove skillet from heat; stir in the rest of the ingredients, except the Parmesan cheese. Spoon mixture into the baking dish.

Bake for 25 minutes. Remove the casserole from the oven; top with the Parmesan cheese. Continue baking for 5-10 minutes, until the casserole is bubbly and the cheese is melted.

Note: Individual baking dishes can be used instead of one large baking dish. Adjust baking time accordingly.

Outpost Inn

Located on 40 acres facing the Continental Divide, The Outpost Bed and Breakfast Inn is a getaway for a weekend, a week or more in the heart of one of Colorado's most beautiful and affordable resorts.

During ski season, guests of The Outpost Inn enjoy free shuttle service to the ski areas of Winter Park and Mary Jane. For cross-country skiing enthusiasts, Devil's Thumb and Idlewild nordic centers are nearby.

INNKEEPERS:	Barbara Parker
ADDRESS:	PO Box 41
	Winter Park, CO 80482
TELEPHONE:	(970) 726-5346; (800) 430-4538
E-MAIL:	barbarajane@winterparkweb.com
WEBSITE:	www.winterpark-inn.com
ROOMS:	7 Rooms; All with private baths
CHILDREN:	Welcome
ANIMALS:	Not allowed; Resident pets
HANDICAPPED:	Not handicapped accessible
DIETARY NEEDS:	Will accommodate guests' special dietary needs

Penne Provençal

Makes 6 Servings

1	large green bell pepper
1	large red bell pepper
½	large Spanish onion
¼	cup olive oil
12	Roma tomatoes, chopped
1	(12-ounce) can butter beans, drained
¼	cup coarsely chopped fresh basil
1	pound penne pasta

Slice the green and red peppers and onion into strips. Heat the olive oil in a skillet and sauté the bell peppers and onion until the onion is translucent. Add the tomatoes; cover and simmer slowly on low for 20 minutes. Add the drained beans and chopped basil. Cover and simmer 20 minutes more. Meanwhile, bring a pot of water to a boil and cook the pasta according the package directions to al dente. Serve the sauce over the pasta.

> *✿ Carol's Corner*
> *A beautiful blend of colors and flavors – a dinner sure to please your vegetarian friends! If you prefer your vegetables crisp-tender, shorten the simmering time. For a finishing touch, garnish with some chopped fresh parsley and finely shredded fresh Parmesan cheese.*

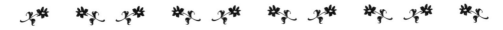

Sky Valley Lodge

Warm weather activities at Sky Valley Lodge include hiking, biking, hot air balloon rides and rodeos. Winter guests enjoy downhill skiing and snowmobiling. For the cross-country skiing enthusiast, the famous ski trail, Devil's Hangover, ends at the lodge.

Complimentary gourmet continental breakfasts are served daily in the dining room. A special "kiddy" nook provides diversions for children.

INNKEEPERS:	Jerry LaSage
ADDRESS:	31490 East Highway 40; PO Box 3132
	Steamboat Springs, CO 80477
TELEPHONE:	(970) 879-7749; (800) 538-7519
E-MAIL:	info@steamboat-lodging.com
WEBSITE:	www.steamboat-lodging.com
ROOMS:	12 Rooms; All with private baths
CHILDREN:	Welcome
ANIMALS:	Not allowed
HANDICAPPED:	Not handicapped accessible
DIETARY NEEDS:	Cannot accommodate guests' special dietary needs

Backyard B.B.Q. Soup

Makes 8 Servings

Use your grill to roast the vegetables for this soup.

3-4	heads (bulbs) garlic
10	cups vegetable broth
½	cup sun-dried tomato pesto (available at more groceries)
1½	tablespoons sugar

Salt and pepper to taste

1	head cauliflower
1	eggplant
1	large onion
3	red bell peppers
10	plum tomatoes
3	ears corn

Preheat oven to 350°F. Bake garlic until tender (see *Carol's Corner*). Meanwhile, heat vegetable broth with pesto, sugar, salt and pepper. When garlic is done, cool a bit, then squeeze out cloves and mash with a fork. Add to the broth. Cut cauliflower, eggplant, onion and peppers into large pieces. Cut tomatoes in half lengthwise. Grill vegetables until there are dark grill marks on all sides (but watch carefully so they don't burn). Chop the grilled vegetables into bite-size pieces and cut corn from ears; add to the stock. Bring soup to a boil, lower heat, simmer for 15 minutes and serve.

⚘ *Carol's Corner*

If you have never tried baked garlic, you are in for a real treat! Be sure to bake some extra bulbs, so that you have some left over to spread on French bread. When baked, garlic becomes very rich and mellow, without any sharpness to its flavor.

To Bake Garlic: Cut about 1/4-inch off the top of each bulb to expose the garlic in the individual cloves. Place the bulbs, cut side up, on foil. Drizzle each bulb with 1-2 teaspoons of olive oil. Sprinkle with a little salt and pepper, if desired. Fold the foil securely around the garlic. Bake at 350°F for about 45 minutes, or until the garlic is soft and tender. Cool slightly and gently squeeze the garlic out of the cloves. Spread on bread or use in recipes.

Allenspark Lodge

Nestled in a quiet village near Rocky Mountain National Park, the Allenspark Lodge boasts comfortable guestrooms, a magnificent great room and a spacious sun room that is perfect for meetings, receptions and weddings.

A hot, family-style breakfast is served each morning. Wine, local micro-brew beers and soft drinks are available for late afternoon enjoyment.

INNKEEPERS:	Bill & Juanita Martin
ADDRESS:	PO Box 247
	Allenspark, CO 80510
TELEPHONE:	(303) 747-2552
E-MAIL:	info@allensparklodge.com
WEBSITE:	www.allensparklodge.com
ROOMS:	14 Rooms; Private & shared baths
CHILDREN:	Children age 14 and older are welcome
ANIMALS:	Not allowed
HANDICAPPED:	Not handicapped accessible
DIETARY NEEDS:	Will accommodate guests' special dietary needs

Spicy Sausage Potato Soup

Makes 4 to 6 Servings

Very flavorful, yet made with ease. This hearty soup makes a complete meal when paired with a tossed green salad. Remember this recipe when you have leftover potatoes and you'll have a head start on lunch or dinner.

1	pound spicy bulk sausage (Italian or breakfast sausage)
½	cup thinly sliced onion
½	cup chopped celery
1-2	teaspoons Montreal steak seasoning (or similar seasoning)
2-3	cups milk
3	large potatoes, cooked and sliced (or cubed)

In a stockpot or large skillet, brown the sausage. Add the onions and celery; sauté until sausage is thoroughly cooked and onions are translucent.

Drain any fat. Add the seasoning, milk and cooked potatoes.

Bring all ingredients to a slow boil; lower heat and simmer for 15-20 minutes. Ladle into soup bowls.

Desserts

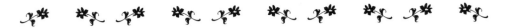

Ambiance Inn

The Ambiance Inn is within walking distance of downtown Carbondale, a small mountain community located at the base of Mt. Sopris. Breakfast is served in the dining room and although the meat and egg recipes vary, guests can always count on the freshly baked original breads.

Accommodations are superior, including the Aspen Suite, Sonoma Room, Santa Fe Room and the Kauai Room, all with private baths and each with its own special ambiance.

INNKEEPERS:	Bob & Norma Morris
ADDRESS:	66 North Second Street; Carbondale, CO 81623
TELEPHONE:	(970) 963-3597; (800) 350-1515
E-MAIL:	ambiancein@aol.com
WEBSITE:	www.ambianceinn.com
ROOMS:	4 Rooms; Private baths
CHILDREN:	Children 7 and older are welcome
ANIMALS:	Not allowed
HANDICAPPED:	Not handicapped accessible
DIETARY NEEDS:	Will accommodate guests' special dietary needs

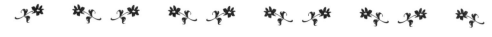

Chocolate Carrot Cake

Makes 12 Servings

2   cups flour
1½   cups sugar
1   cup vegetable oil
½   cup orange juice
¼   cup unsweetened cocoa
2   teaspoons baking soda
1   teaspoon salt
1   teaspoon cinnamon
1   teaspoon vanilla
4   eggs
2   cups shredded carrots
1   (3.5-ounce) package (1⅓ cups) shredded coconut
Glaze or icing

Preheat oven to 350°F. In a large bowl, mix, at low speed, all of the ingredients, except the carrots and coconut, until well blended, scraping often. Increase speed to high for 2 minutes. Stir in carrots and coconut. Spoon into greased and floured Bundt pan. Bake for 50-55 minutes, or until a toothpick inserted in the center comes out clean. Cool on wire rack for 10-15 minutes, then remove from pan. Glaze or ice the cooled cake.

Variation: Bake the cake in a greased and floured 13x9-inch baking pan for 35-45 minutes. Cool completely. Frost with cream cheese frosting (recipe below). Store in refrigerator.

Cream cheese frosting:
1   (3-ounce) package cream cheese
6   tablespoons (¾ stick) butter, room temperature
1   tablespoon milk
1   teaspoon vanilla extract
3   cups powdered sugar

Heat together cream cheese, butter, milk and vanilla until smooth. Off the heat, gradually add powdered sugar. Beat until smooth.

St. Mary's Glacier

St. Mary's Glacier Bed and Breakfast, at 10,500 feet, is the highest B&B in North America. It borders Arapahoe National Forest and the historic silver and gold rush routes. Guests enjoy such activities as hiking, mountain biking, cross-country and world-class downhill skiing.

Surrounded by snow-capped Continental Divide peaks, a cascading waterfall and crystalline high mountain lakes, the inn is just a short hike from the southernmost glacier in North America.

INNKEEPERS:	Iyad Allis
ADDRESS:	336 Crest Drive
	Idaho Springs, CO 80452
TELEPHONE:	(303) 567-4084
E-MAIL:	glacierbb@yahoo.com
WEBSITE:	www.stmarysglacierbb.com
ROOMS:	7 Rooms; All with private baths
CHILDREN:	Not allowed
ANIMALS:	Not allowed
HANDICAPPED:	Not handicapped accessible
DIETARY NEEDS:	Will accommodate guests' special dietary needs

Bacardi Rum Cake

Makes 12 Servings

This is consistently one of the most popular recipes in the Colorado Bed & Breakfast Cookbook.

½   cup chopped pecans or walnuts
1   (18½-ounce) package yellow cake mix (without pudding in the mix)
1   (3.4-ounce) package Jell-O instant vanilla pudding mix
4   eggs
¼   cup cold water
½   cup vegetable oil
½   cup Bacardi light or dark rum, 80 proof

Preheat oven to 325°F. Grease and flour 10-inch tube or 12-cup Bundt pan. Sprinkle nuts over bottom of pan. Mix the rest of the cake ingredients together. Pour batter over nuts. Bake about 1 hour. Cool for approximately 30 minutes and invert onto serving plate. Make glaze while cake is cooling. Prick all over top of baked cake with a toothpick. Drizzle and smooth glaze evenly over top and sides, allowing glaze to soak into cake. Keep spooning the glaze over the cake until all of the glaze has been absorbed.

Glaze:
½   cup (1 stick) butter
¼   cup water
1   cup sugar
½   cup Bacardi rum

Melt butter in a medium saucepan. Stir in water and sugar. Boil for 5 minutes, stirring constantly. Remove from heat and cool slightly. slowly stir in the rum, so it doesn't splatter. While warm, spoon over cake.

Lavender Swing

Comfortable days and cool, starlit nights epitomize the essence of the Lavender Swing Bed and Breakfast. Located in magical Glenwood Springs, the famous Glenwood Hot Springs Pool is within walking distance of your room.

Local activities include rafting on the Colorado River, fly-fishing on the Colorado River, Roaring Fork River or Fryingpan River, visiting Redstone Castle or touring the historic Marble Mine at Marble Mountain.

INNKEEPERS:	Pat Means & Carolyn Goller
ADDRESS:	802 Palmer Avenue
	Glenwood Springs, CO 81601
TELEPHONE:	(970) 945-8289
E-MAIL:	lavender@rof.net
WEBSITE:	www.lavenderswing.com
ROOMS:	3 Rooms; All with private baths
CHILDREN:	Children age 15 and older are welcome
ANIMALS:	Not allowed; Resident parrot "Sally"
HANDICAPPED:	Not handicapped accessible
DIETARY NEEDS:	Will accommodate guests' special dietary needs

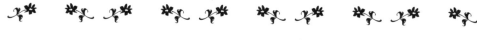

Mixed Berry Pudding Cake

Makes 6 Servings

Imagine the smiles on your guests' faces as you dish up this special, hot fruit dish for breakfast. Or top it with ice cream for a "berry" heartwarming dessert.

2	cups frozen mixed berries (strawberry-blueberry-raspberry-blackberry mix)
1	teaspoon fresh lemon juice
1	teaspoon cinnamon
1	cup all-purpose flour
¾	cup sugar
1	teaspoon baking powder
½	cup 2% milk
3	tablespoons butter, melted

Topping:

¾	cup sugar
1	tablespoon cornstarch
1	cup boiling water

Preheat oven to 350°F. Coat an 8-inch square baking dish with nonstick cooking spray. In a medium bowl, gently mix the frozen berries with the lemon juice and cinnamon. Spread berries evenly in the baking dish.

In another bowl, sift together the flour, sugar and baking powder; stir in the milk and the melted butter. Spoon the batter over the berries.

For the topping, in a small dish, combine the sugar and cornstarch. Sprinkle the mixture evenly over the batter. Pour the boiling water evenly over all of the ingredients. Do not stir. Bake for 45 minutes, or until a toothpick inserted in the center of the cake comes out clean.

Pikes Peak Paradise

This is the place to escape to if you are looking for romantic privacy or a luxurious spot to relax. Let the majestic, towering views of Pikes Peak and the gentle sounds of the whispering pines be your accommodations.

"This is a place where it is easy to catch your breath and listen to your heart. Romance, peace and privacy await you." — Owners, Pikes Peak Paradise

INNKEEPERS:	Rayne & Bart Reese
ADDRESS:	236 Pinecrest Road
	Woodland Park, CO 80863
TELEPHONE:	(719) 687-6656
E-MAIL:	pppbnb@bemail.com
WEBSITE:	www.pikespeakmall.com/pppbandb
ROOMS:	1 Room; 4 Suites; Private & shared baths
CHILDREN:	Children age 10 and older are welcome
ANIMALS:	Well-behaved dogs are welcome; Resident cats
HANDICAPPED:	Not handicapped accessible
DIETARY NEEDS:	Will accommodate guests' special dietary needs

Apple Crisp for Two

Makes 2 Servings

Perfect for a quiet, special evening at home for just the two of you! For a delicious finish, top the apple crisp with whipped cream or ice cream.

1   large apple, peeled, cored and sliced
Juice of ½ lemon, more or less
Salt to taste

Topping:
½   cup packed brown sugar
¼   cup rolled oats (not instant oats)
½   cup graham cracker crumbs
1   teaspoon cinnamon
¼   cup (½ stick) butter, room temperature

Preheat oven to 325°F. Coat a 7x5x2-inch baking dish (or similar size) with nonstick cooking spray. Place the apple slices into the baking dish. Sprinkle with lemon juice and salt.

To make the topping, in a medium bowl, mix together the brown sugar, oats, graham cracker crumbs, cinnamon and softened butter. Sprinkle over the apples.

Bake for 30-45 minutes, or until the apples are tender and the topping is browned and crisp. Serve warm or at room temperature.

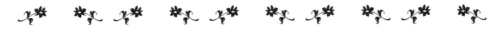

Allenspark Lodge

Since 1933, Allenspark Lodge has woven its special magic for the community and the weary traveler alike. Constructed of native stone and majestic ponderosa pine, its warmth and peacefulness have embraced and renewed its guests throughout the years.

A variety of snacks, hot soups, desserts, wine, beer and soft drinks are offered in the Wilderquest Room. Box lunches are available by advance request.

INNKEEPERS:	Bill & Juanita Martin
ADDRESS:	PO Box 247
	Allenspark, CO 80510
TELEPHONE:	(303) 747-2552
E-MAIL:	info@allensparklodge.com
WEBSITE:	www.allensparklodge.com
ROOMS:	14 Rooms; Private & shared baths
CHILDREN:	Children age 14 and older are welcome
ANIMALS:	Not allowed
HANDICAPPED:	Not handicapped accessible
DIETARY NEEDS:	Will accommodate guests' special dietary needs

Blueberry Pot Pie

Makes 6 to 8 Servings

This "pot pie" is a wonderful dessert, made even better by adding whipped cream or vanilla ice cream.

Filling:

1	(16-ounce) package frozen blueberries
3	tablespoons grape jelly
1	tablespoon flour
1	tablespoon sugar

Preheat oven to 325°F. Coat an 8-inch round baking pan with nonstick cooking spray. Place frozen blueberries in the baking pan. Sprinkle the berries with flour and sugar. Add the grape jelly; toss to combine. Spread evenly in the pan.

Batter and topping:

3	tablespoons butter, room temperature
⅓	cup sugar plus 1 tablespoon for sprinkling on top
1	egg
½	teaspoon vanilla extract
¼	cup sour cream
¾	cup flour
¾	teaspoon baking powder
⅛	teaspoon baking soda
⅛	teaspoon salt
1½	cups chopped pecans

In a large bowl, beat together the butter and ⅓ cup sugar. Add the egg and vanilla, beating until light and fluffy. Beat in the sour cream. Sift together the flour, baking powder, baking soda, and salt. Stir flour mixture into the butter mixture. Fold in the pecans. Drop the batter by spoonfuls over the blueberries. Sprinkle with the 1 tablespoon sugar. Bake for 45-55 minutes, or until the crust is golden brown. Serve hot or at room temperature with whipped cream or ice cream.

Last Resort

The Last Resort Bed and Breakfast is nestled along the scenic banks of Coal Creek in the heart of downtown Crested Butte. This unique and conveniently located lodge features a private library, steam room, spacious solarium with magnificent mountain views, private Jacuzzis and a hearty, all-you-can-eat breakfast.

Extra amenities include guided cross-country skiing and hiking tours. French and Spanish are spoken.

INNKEEPERS:	Rita Wengrin
ADDRESS:	213 Third Street; PO Box 722
	Crested Butte, CO 81224
TELEPHONE:	(970) 349-0445; (800) 349-0445
E-MAIL:	ritawengrin@yahoo.com
WEBSITE:	www.ritaslastresort.com
ROOMS:	7 Rooms; Private & shared baths
CHILDREN:	Children age 12 and over are welcome
ANIMALS:	Not allowed
HANDICAPPED:	Is handicapped accessible
DIETARY NEEDS:	Will accommodate guests' special dietary needs

Apple Walnut Delight

Makes 6 Servings

4   apples (any crisp red apple, such as Braeburn or Gala)
Cinnamon to taste
Nutmeg to taste
½   cup Bisquick
1   cup sugar
2   tablespoons butter, cut into pieces
2   eggs
⅓   cup milk

Preheat oven to 325°F. Peel and core the apples. Slice apples and put them into a medium bowl. Sprinkle some cinnamon and nutmeg over the apples and toss to combine. Place apples into a greased, 10-inch deep dish pie pan.

In a mixing bowl, beat together the Bisquick, sugar, butter, eggs and milk Pour mixture over the apples.

Sprinkle streusel topping over batter and apples. Bake for about 1 hour. Serve with a dollop of whipped cream and a slice of apple for garnish. Equally good for breakfast or dinner.

Streusel topping:
1   cup Bisquick
½   cup chopped walnuts
⅓   cup packed brown sugar
3   tablespoons cold butter, cut into pieces

Make the streusel topping by combining the Bisquick, walnuts, brown sugar and cold butter by hand.

> *Carol's Corner*
>
> *This is something similar to apple pie – except you don't have to make a crust. Try serving it warm with a big scoop of vanilla ice cream.*

Ice Palace Inn

The history of the Ice Palace Inn Bed and Breakfast began 100 years ago when the city of Leadville built the famous Leadville Ice Palace to bolster a sagging economy. The Ice Palace took 36 days to construct and covered five acres. Constructed of 5,000 tons of ice and 307,000 board feet of lumber, it was the largest ice palace ever built in North America.

When the Ice Palace closed in 1896, some of its lumber was used in 1899 to construct what is today's Ice Palace Inn.

INNKEEPERS:	Giles & Kami Kolakowski
ADDRESS:	813 Spruce Street
	Leadville, CO 80461
TELEPHONE:	(719) 486-8272; (800) 754-2840
E-MAIL:	icepalace@bwn.net
WEBSITE:	www.icepalaceinn.com
ROOMS:	5 Rooms; All with private baths
CHILDREN:	Welcome
ANIMALS:	Not allowed
HANDICAPPED:	Not handicapped accessible
DIETARY NEEDS:	Will accommodate guests' special dietary needs

Very Berry Pie

Makes One (9-inch) Pie, 8 Servings

Delicious with ice cream!

1½   cups blueberries
1½   cups raspberries
1   cup blackberries
1   cup sugar
3   tablespoons quick-cooking tapioca
Pastry for double-crust 9-inch pie (unbaked)
2-3 tablespoons butter
Cinnamon-sugar (2 teaspoons sugar mixed with ⅛ teaspoon cinnamon)

In a large bowl, mix together the blueberries, raspberries, blackberries, sugar and tapioca. Let stand for 15 minutes.

Preheat oven to 400°F. Line an ungreased 9-inch pie pan with one pastry. Fill the pastry-lined pie pan with the berry mixture. Dot the top of the fruit with small pieces of butter. Place the remaining pastry over the filling. Seal edges; crimp as desired. Cut a few slits in the top pastry to allow steam to escape during baking. Sprinkle the top of the unbaked pie with the cinnamon-sugar mixture.

Bake for 45-60 minutes, until juices form bubbles that burst slowly. Cool pie on a wire rack for 3 to 4 hours to allow the pie to set up before serving.

River Run Inn

L isted on the National Register of Historic Places, the River Run Inn was built in 1892 as the Chaffee County poor farm. Today, it bears little resemblance to its humble beginnings. A gracious front porch is a favorite place for guests to enjoy their morning coffee.

The inn's delightful country setting and spaciousness makes it a favorite for family reunions, weddings, romantic getaways and outdoor enthusiasts.

INNKEEPERS:	Virginia Nemmers
ADDRESS:	8495 County Road 160
	Salida, CO 81201
TELEPHONE:	(719) 539-3818
E-MAIL:	riverrun@amigo.net
WEBSITE:	www.riverruninn.com
ROOMS:	8 Rooms; All with private baths
CHILDREN:	Children age 10 and older are welcome
ANIMALS:	Not allowed; Resident dog
HANDICAPPED:	Not handicapped accessible
DIETARY NEEDS:	Will accommodate guests' special dietary needs

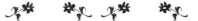

Peanut Butter Fudge Ice Cream Pie

Makes One (9-inch) Pie, About 6 Servings

Peanut butter and chocolate – a classic combination that's hard to beat! Be sure to bake and cool the crust before you mix the ice cream and peanut butter.

1   (9-inch) graham cracker crust
1   quart vanilla ice cream, softened
½   cup peanut butter
Hot fudge topping (about ⅔ cup)

Following the package or recipe directions, bake the graham cracker crust until golden; set aside to cool completely. In a large mixing bowl, combine the softened ice cream with the peanut butter. Beat until thoroughly mixed (or leave the mixture somewhat swirled, if you prefer).

Layer half of the ice cream mixture in the cooled crust. Drizzle with half of the hot fudge. (Place the pie in the freezer for 10 minutes if you need to firm the ice cream and topping before adding the next layer.) Spread remaining ice cream on top and drizzle with the remaining hot fudge.

Immediately place the ice cream pie, uncovered, in the freezer for 30 minutes. Remove pie from freezer and cover with foil or plastic wrap. Return pie to freezer and keep frozen until using (the pie will be easier to cut if you take it out of the freezer 10-15 minutes before serving).

⁂ Carol's Corner

To help level the ice cream layers in the crust, place waxed paper over the ice cream and press down gently with your fingers.

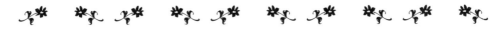

Porter House

The Porter House Bed and Breakfast was built in the Queen Anne Victorian style by Dr. Frank Porter, a respected physician and surgeon in the Windsor community. The Windsor Leader newspaper reported, "Dr. Porter's magnificent residence is the prettiest house in northern Colorado."

The Porter House is the perfect setting for corporate retreats, business conferences, seminars, wedding receptions or any special occasion.

INNKEEPERS:	Tom & Marni Schmittling
ADDRESS:	530 Main Street
	Windsor, CO 80550
TELEPHONE:	(970) 686-5793
E-MAIL:	phbbinn@aol.com
WEBSITE:	www.bbonline.com/co/porterhouse
ROOMS:	4 Rooms; 1 Suite; All with private baths
CHILDREN:	Children 14 and older are welcome
ANIMALS:	Not allowed
HANDICAPPED:	Not handicapped accessible
DIETARY NEEDS:	Will accommodate guests' special dietary needs

Porter House Oatmeal Cranberry Cookies

Makes 7 to 8 Dozen Cookies

1	cup butter (2 sticks), room temperature
1	cup packed brown sugar
2	eggs
2	cups all-purpose flour
1½	teaspoons baking soda
2	cups rolled oats (not instant oats)
1½	cups dried cranberries
1½	cups white chocolate chips
½	cup chopped walnuts (optional)

Preheat oven to 375°F. Lightly grease a baking sheet. Beat together the butter and brown sugar. Add eggs and mix until combined. Stir in the flour, baking soda and oatmeal. Stir in the cranberries, chips and nuts.

Use a cookie scoop for evenly sized cookies, or drop by rounded tablespoon onto lightly greased baking sheet. Bake for 10-12 minutes. Let stand for about 2 minutes; remove to wire rack to cool completely.

Boulder Victoria

D. SPRINGER '90 ©

O ne of Boulder's grandest original homes, the Boulder Victoria is a historic 1870's landmark that has been meticulously renovated. The recipient of Historic Boulder's Preservation Award and the City of Boulder's Landscape Design Award, it has been featured in *Country Living* magazine and *Bon Appétit* magazine.

Afternoon tea includes scones, lemon curd, shortbread and cakes. Evening port in the parlor provides a soothing conclusion to the day's activities.

INNKEEPERS:	Lupita Dudley
ADDRESS:	1305 Pine Street
	Boulder, CO 80302
TELEPHONE:	(303) 938-1300
E-MAIL:	www.bouldervictoria.com/reservations_form.html
WEBSITE:	www.bouldervictoria.com
ROOMS:	5 Rooms; 2 Suites; All with private baths
CHILDREN:	Children age 12 and older are welcome
ANIMALS:	Not allowed
HANDICAPPED:	Not handicapped accessible
DIETARY NEEDS:	Will accommodate guests' special dietary needs

Kristen's Mocha Chip Cookies

Makes 8 Dozen Cookies

These cookies are especially good served warm, when they are still nice and chewy!

2½   cups semi-sweet chocolate chips, divided
1   cup (2 sticks) butter, room temperature
1   cup packed brown sugar
1   cup white sugar
2   eggs
4   teaspoons hot water
4   tablespoons instant coffee granules
2   teaspoons vanilla extract
3   cups all-purpose flour
1½   teaspoons baking soda
½   teaspoon salt
Powdered sugar

Melt 1 cup of the chocolate chips over low heat and set aside. In a large bowl, cream together butter, brown sugar and white sugar. Add the eggs and mix until smooth. Stir coffee granules into hot water until dissolved; stir into the butter mixture, along with the vanilla. Mix in the melted chocolate.

In small bowl, combine flour, baking soda and salt. Gradually stir this into the butter mixture. Blend in remaining 1½ cups chocolate chips. Refrigerate dough until stiff.

Preheat oven to 350°F. Form chilled dough into small balls and roll in powdered sugar. Place on an ungreased cookie sheet and bake for about 8-10 minutes. Remove from oven when surface appears "cracked" and dough has spread somewhat, but is not yet flat.

Inn on Mapleton Hill

Located on a quiet, residential street in Boulder's grandest historic neighborhood, the Inn on Mapleton Hill has been a welcoming haven since 1899 when Emma Clark, a widowed dressmaker and daughter of a Canadian sea captain, took in boarders, including many school teachers.

Mapleton Hill, with its towering maple and cottonwood trees and its turn-of-the-twentieth-century mansions, is a wonderful place to stroll or bike.

INNKEEPERS:	Judi & Ray Schultze
ADDRESS:	1001 Spruce Street
	Boulder, CO 80302
TELEPHONE:	(303) 449-6528
E-MAIL:	maphillinn@aol.com
WEBSITE:	www.innonmapletonhill.com
ROOMS:	7 Rooms; 2 Suites; Private & shared baths
CHILDREN:	Children age 12 and older are welcome
ANIMALS:	Not allowed
HANDICAPPED:	Not handicapped accessible
DIETARY NEEDS:	Will accommodate guests' special dietary needs

Inn on Mapleton Hill's Signature Chocolate Chip Cookies

Makes About 4½ Dozen Cookies

"This is a variation on a simple chocolate chip cookie which I've developed by simply watching how fast they disappear from the cookie jar. I first realized these were a major hit when I filled the cookie jar one night just before bed and came in the next morning to find it totally empty! There's been many a midnight raid on the cookie jar since!" — Judi Schultze, Inn on Mapleton Hill

1	cup (2 sticks) butter, room temperature
¾	cup packed brown sugar
¾	cup white sugar
2	extra large eggs
3	teaspoons vanilla extract
2½	cups all-purpose flour
1	generous teaspoon baking soda
1	teaspoon salt

Finely grated zest of 2 large oranges

2	cups semi-sweet chocolate chips
2	cups rolled oats (not instant oats)

Preheat oven to 375°F. In a large bowl, cream together butter and both sugars. Add eggs and vanilla; beat until creamy. Sift together flour, baking soda and salt. Gradually mix the dry ingredients into the wet ingredients. Add orange zest, chocolate chips and oats. Mix well (dough will be stiff).

Drop small spoonfuls of the dough on a preheated baking stone (the stone prevents the cookie bottoms from burning and allows the cookies to bake more evenly). (The cookies may also be baked on an insulated cookie sheet using parchment paper, or a greased baking sheet.)

Bake for about 13 minutes. Remove cookies to a wire rack. When cooled, store in an airtight container. Cookies freeze well.

Manor

The majestic mountains that surround the Manor Bed and Breakfast provide guests with some of the most spectacular hiking, mountain biking and Jeep trails that are accessible in Colorado. Guests can ski Telluride for half-price or soak in the hot springs for free.

Guestrooms are tastefully decorated with Victorian furnishings. Each of the seven rooms is located on the second or third floor, with commanding views of the surrounding mountains.

INNKEEPERS:	John & Kay Gowins
ADDRESS:	317 Second Street; PO Box 1165
	Ouray, CO 81427
TELEPHONE:	(970) 325-4574
E-MAIL:	themanor@ouraycolorado.net
WEBSITE:	www.ouraycolorado.com
ROOMS:	7 Rooms; All with private baths
CHILDREN:	Can accommodate one child age 5 or older
ANIMALS:	Not allowed
HANDICAPPED:	Is handicapped accessible
DIETARY NEEDS:	Will accommodate guests' special dietary needs

Wholesome Wheatgerm Oatmeal Cookies

Makes 3 Dozen Large Cookies

"Served at our afternoon tea, these nutty-textured cookies are a favorite. They also pack well for our guests, who take advantage of the numerous hiking trails in the local mountains. A healthy treat!" — Diane Kramer, Manor B&B

1⅓	cups margarine
2	teaspoons vanilla extract
2	cups packed brown sugar (can reduce to 1 cup for reduced calories)
2	eggs
2	cups all-purpose flour
1½	teaspoons salt
1	teaspoon baking soda
1	teaspoon cinnamon
1½	cups wheat germ
4½	cups rolled oats (not instant oats)
1½	cups raisins

Preheat oven to 350°F. In a very large bowl, cream the margarine, vanilla, brown sugar and eggs. In a medium bowl, sift together the flour, salt, baking soda and cinnamon. Stir in the wheat germ. Add the the wet ingredients and mix together. Stir in the oats and raisins.

Spoon 2-inch mounds of dough onto a lightly greased baking sheet. Bake for 12-15 minutes, or until golden brown. Store cookies in an airtight container. Cookies freeze well.

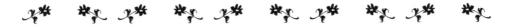

Logwood

G uests of Logwood Bed and Breakfast enjoy the glorious fall color change of the Colorado aspen trees. Other activities include riding in a horse-drawn sleigh, soaking in the famous Trimble Hot Springs or taking Jeep rides into the magnificent Rocky Mountains.

"Delightful, lovely, attractive … guests can only come away with wonderful memories" — National Bed & Breakfast Association

INNKEEPERS:	The Windmuellers
ADDRESS:	35060 U.S. Highway 550 North
	Durango, CO 81301
TELEPHONE:	(970) 259-4396; (800) 369-4082
E-MAIL:	paul@durango-logwoodinn.com
WEBSITE:	www.durango-logwoodinn.com
ROOMS:	7 Rooms; 2 Suites; All with private baths
CHILDREN:	Welcome
ANIMALS:	Not allowed; Resident cats
HANDICAPPED:	Not handicapped accessible
DIETARY NEEDS:	Will accommodate guests' special dietary needs

Best Oatmeal Sour Cream Chocolate Chip Cookies

Makes 5½ Dozen

2	cups all-purpose flour
1	teaspoon baking soda
½	teaspoon salt
1	cup rolled oats (not instant oats)
1¼	cups packed light brown sugar
1	cup (2 sticks) unsalted butter, room temperature
2	eggs
1	teaspoon vanilla extract
½	cup sour cream
12	ounces (2 cups) semi-sweet chocolate chips
12	ounces (2 cups) milk chocolate chips
¼	cup raisins (coarsely chopped)
¾	cup dried cherries or dried cranberries
¾	cup chopped walnuts

Preheat oven to 350°F. In a medium bowl, sift flour, baking soda and salt together; stir in rolled oats. Set aside. In a large bowl, cream together the sugar and butter until light and fluffy. Beat in eggs and vanilla. Stir sifted ingredients into creamed mixture until just combined. Mix in sour cream until just blended. Stir in chocolate chips, raisins, dried cherries and nuts.

Drop heaping teaspoons of dough onto ungreased baking sheets, placing cookies 2 inches apart. Bake for 12-15 minutes, or until slightly browned around the edges. Allow to cool on baking sheets for 5 minutes before removing to wire racks to cool completely.

Conejos Ranch

The Conejos River, a fisherman's paradise, runs through the Conejos Ranch. The soothing sound of the river helps guests relax, read, meditate or just ponder life.

The proprietor of the Conejos Ranch wrote about an evening when a little girl started crying. He asked, "What's wrong?" The little girl replied, "Tomorrow my family is leaving here and we have to go to Disney World!"

INNKEEPERS:	Ms. Shorty Fry
ADDRESS:	25390 Highway 17
	Antonito, CO 81120
TELEPHONE:	(719) 376-2464
E-MAIL:	info@conejosranch.com
WEBSITE:	www.conejosranch.com.com
ROOMS:	8 Rooms; All with private baths; 6 Log Cabins
CHILDREN:	Welcome
ANIMALS:	Welcome
HANDICAPPED:	Handicapped accessible
DIETARY NEEDS:	Will accommodate guests' special dietary needs

Conejos Cookies

Makes 6 Dozen Cookies

"We try to have these in the rooms when our guests arrive! We also put them in our boxed lunches." — Janna Nail, Conejos River Ranch

1	cup (2 sticks) butter, room temperature
1	cup white sugar
1	cup packed brown sugar
1	egg
1	cup vegetable oil
1	tablespoon vanilla extract
1	cup rolled oats (not instant oats)
1	cup Rice Krispies
½	cup shredded coconut
½	cup chopped toasted pecans
3½	cups all-purpose flour
1	teaspoon baking soda
1	teaspoon salt

Preheat oven to 325°F. Cream butter, sugar and brown sugar until light and fluffy. Add egg, vegetable oil and vanilla. Mix well. Add oats, Rice Krispies, coconut and pecans. Stir well. Sift together flour, baking soda and salt, and stir into the other ingredients until well blended. Drop by teaspoonfuls on greased insulated cookie sheets (they keep the cookies from getting too brown on the bottom). Bake for approximately 15 minutes.

Holden House

This storybook, Colonial Revival Victorian home and carriage house was built in 1902 by Mrs. Isabel Holden, widow of businessman and rancher Daniel M. Holden. The Holdens owned mining interests in Aspen, Cripple Creek, Leadville, Silverton, Goldfield and Independence.

The Holden House - 1902 Bed and Breakfast Inn was restored in the mid-1980's and has been filled with the Clarks' antiques and family heirlooms.

INNKEEPERS:	Sallie & Welling Clark
ADDRESS:	1102 West Pikes Peak Avenue
	Colorado Springs, CO 80904
TELEPHONE:	(719) 471-3980
E-MAIL:	mail@holdenhouse.com
WEBSITE:	www.holdenhouse.com
ROOMS:	5 Suites; All with private baths
CHILDREN:	Not allowed
ANIMALS:	Not allowed
HANDICAPPED:	Is handicapped accessible
DIETARY NEEDS:	Will accommodate guests' special dietary needs

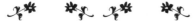

Chocolate Chunk White Chocolate Chip Cookies

Makes 2 Dozen Cookies

"A favorite for afternoon tea. The Holden House's bottomless cookie jar is always a hit with our bed and breakfast guests." — *Sallie Clark, Holden House*

¾	cup packed brown sugar
¾	cup (1½ sticks) butter or margarine
2	eggs
1	teaspoon vanilla extract
2½	cups all-purpose flour
1	teaspoon baking soda
6	ounces (1 cup) chocolate chunks
6	ounces (1 cup) Hershey's vanilla chips
¼	cup chopped walnuts

Preheat oven to 375°F. Microwave brown sugar and butter in a medium microwaveable bowl for 1 minute on high. Remove from microwave and stir in eggs and vanilla. Add flour and baking soda to sugar/egg mixture. When well mixed, stir in chocolate chunks, vanilla chips and walnuts. Place well rounded teaspoons of dough on an ungreased, insulated cookie sheet (it keeps cookies from getting too brown on the bottom). Bake for 10-12 minutes, or until slightly brown on top.

Anniversary Inn

Nestled on three acres of spruce and pine trees, the Anniversary Inn Bed and Breakfast provides a comfortable atmosphere for adults seeking a quiet getaway. Each guestroom in this 100-year-old log inn is named after a Strauss Waltz. The Sweethearts Cottage, a favorite of honeymoon and anniversary couples, boasts a fireplace and jetted tub-for-two.

A bountiful breakfast is served in a glass-enclosed porch and includes fruit, freshly baked goods and a delicious entrée.

INNKEEPERS:	Trish & Walt Hebert
ADDRESS:	1060 Mary's Lake Road
	Estes Park, CO 80517
TELEPHONE:	(970) 586-6200
E-MAIL:	thebert@gte.net
WEBSITE:	www.bestinns.net
ROOMS:	3 Rooms; 1 Cottage; All with private baths
CHILDREN:	Call ahead
ANIMALS:	Not allowed
HANDICAPPED:	Not handicapped accessible
DIETARY NEEDS:	Will accommodate guests' special dietary needs

Chocolate Oatmeal Bonbons

Makes 3 Dozen Cookies

A great chocolate treat.

½   cup (1 stick) butter, room temperature
1   egg
1   cup sugar
½   cup unsweetened cocoa powder
¾   cup all-purpose flour
½   teaspoon salt
1   teaspoon baking powder
1¼   cups rolled oats (not instant oats)
1½   teaspoons vanilla extract

Preheat the oven to 350°F. In a large bowl, cream together the butter, egg and sugar. In a small bowl, sift together the cocoa powder, flour, salt and baking powder. Stir the cocoa mixture into the butter/egg mixture. Add the oats and vanilla extract; mix well.

Chill the dough for 1-2 hours. Roll the dough into 1-inch balls. Place the balls 1 to 2 inches apart on a greased baking sheet. Bake for approximately 10 minutes. Remove the cookies from the baking sheet and allow to cool on a wire rack. Store cookies in an airtight covered container.

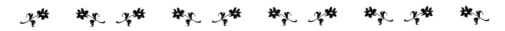

Ice Palace Inn

Located in historic Leadville, the Ice Palace Inn boasts six romantic guestrooms elegantly decorated with antiques, collectibles, Ice Palace mementos and antique quilts. Some rooms have views of Mount Massive and Turquoise Lake. All have feather beds and exquisite private baths.

Afternoon tea, coffee, hot chocolate and goodies are available daily and can be enjoyed in the parlor in front of the fireplace or in the game room where there is always a puzzle in progress.

INNKEEPERS:	Giles & Kami Kolakowski
ADDRESS:	813 Spruce Street
	Leadville, CO 80461
TELEPHONE:	(719) 486-8272; (800) 754-2840
E-MAIL:	icepalace@bwn.net
WEBSITE:	www.icepalaceinn.com
ROOMS:	5 Rooms; All with private baths
CHILDREN:	Welcome
ANIMALS:	Not allowed
HANDICAPPED:	Not handicapped accessible
DIETARY NEEDS:	Will accommodate guests' special dietary needs

Fudgie Scotchie Squares

Makes 81 Small Pieces

Is it a candy, or is it a cookie? Whatever it is, it's a delicious, rich morsel that will satisfy any sweet tooth. It's quick and easy – the hardest part is waiting for them to completely cool before eating!

1½	cups graham cracker crumbs
1	(14-ounce) can Eagle Brand sweetened condensed milk
1	cup semi-sweet chocolate chips
1	cup butterscotch chips
1	cup chopped walnuts

Preheat oven to 350°F. Generously butter a 9-inch square baking pan. In a large bowl, combine all ingredients. Mix thoroughly. Press mixture into the prepared pan.

Bake for 25-30 minutes. Let cool thoroughly! Do not try to cut into squares until completely set. Refrigerate, if desired, to speed cooling. Cut into 1-inch squares. Freezes well.

Our Hearts Inn

Our Hearts Inn, located in Old Colorado City, is a 100-year-old inn with arches and curved ceilings on the first floor. Cowboy and Western stenciling, antiques, hearts, bunnies and rocking chairs (no room is complete without one) give a nostalgic glimpse of the past.

Guests can stroll the tree-lined, streets of boutique and antique shops in Old Colorado City, the restored historic district of Colorado Springs.

INNKEEPERS:	Andy & Pat Fejedelem
ADDRESS:	2215 West Colorado Avenue
	Colorado Springs, CO 80904
TELEPHONE:	(719) 473-8684; (800) 533-7095
E-MAIL:	Not available
WEBSITE:	www.inn-colorado-springs.com
ROOMS:	3 Rooms; All with private baths; 1 Cottage
CHILDREN:	Welcome
ANIMALS:	Not allowed
HANDICAPPED:	Not handicapped accessible
DIETARY NEEDS:	Will accommodate guests' special dietary needs

Andy & Pat's Favorite Fudge

Makes 5 Pounds of Fudge

This rich and creamy fudge recipe is one of Pat's "old family favorites." It makes a large batch – plenty for gift-giving, with enough leftover for family treats!

4	cups sugar
1	(12-ounce) can evaporated milk
1	cup (2 sticks) butter
1	(12-ounce) package (2 cups) semi-sweet chocolate chips
1	(13-ounce) jar marshmallow crème
1	teaspoon vanilla extract
1	cup chopped nuts (optional)

Butter a 13x9-inch baking pan; set aside. In a large, heavy saucepan, combine the sugar, evaporated milk and butter. Bring the mixture to a boil over medium to medium-high heat. Cook, stirring constantly, to the "soft ball" stage (234-238°F on a candy thermometer). Be patient; this step can take up to 20 minutes.

Remove from heat and add the chocolate chips, marshmallow crème, vanilla and nuts. Stir until well blended. Promptly pour the mixture into the baking pan. Let set up and cut into squares. The fudge keeps well in an airtight container. Refrigerate for firm fudge, or serve at room temperature for a softer, creamier texture. The fudge may also be frozen.

B&B
Potpourri

Crystal Dreams

Located in historic Redstone, the Crystal Dreams Bed and Breakfast is a romantic country Victorian home snuggled between majestic red cliffs and the Crystal River.

Redstone is a winter wonderland, offering winter sports enthusiasts cross-country skiing and snowshoeing. For the avid Alpine skier or snowboarder, Aspen is a one hour drive. During the Christmas season, guests can enjoy sleigh rides, and sled dog races are held every January.

INNKEEPERS:	Lisa & Steve Wagner
ADDRESS:	0475 Redstone Boulevard
	Redstone, CO 81623
TELEPHONE:	(970) 963-8240
E-MAIL:	redstone@rof.net
WEBSITE:	www.redstonecolorado.com/crystaldreams
ROOMS:	3 Rooms; All with private baths
CHILDREN:	Children 12 and older are welcome
ANIMALS:	Not allowed
HANDICAPPED:	Not handicapped accessible
DIETARY NEEDS:	Will accommodate guests' special dietary needs

Crystal Dreams
Hot Artichoke Dip

Makes 5 Cups

This is a perfect recipe for the busy hostess ... it can be prepared in advance, and it will feed a crowd!

2   (14-ounce) cans artichoke hearts, drained and chopped
1   (14-ounce) can chopped green chiles
¾   cup mayonnaise
¼   cup sour cream
1   cup grated Parmesan cheese
Garlic (to taste), minced
1   onion, chopped
Chopped parsley for garnish
Crackers or sourdough bread for serving

In a microwaveable serving dish, mix all of the ingredients together, except the chopped parsley (if a thinner consistency is desired, add a little more sour cream). Heat the mixture in the microwave for approximately 2 minutes. Stir to blend. Cover and refrigerate for at least 2 hours.

When ready to serve, reheat in the microwave for 2 to 3 minutes, or until hot. Garnish with a sprinkling of chopped parsley. Serve with crackers or thin slices of sourdough bread.

Mt. Sopris Inn

The Mt. Sopris Inn sits on 14 acres above the Crystal River. A bald eagle and peregrine falcon preserve are within view as is the Perry Ranch, one of the oldest working ranches in Colorado. A nearby fish hatchery produces rainbow trout for the area's rivers.

The breakfast table is set with bone china. Guests enjoy such tasty morning treats as Eggs Benedict and whole grain pancakes.

INNKEEPERS:	Barbara Fasching
ADDRESS:	0165 Mt. Sopris Ranch Road; PO Box 126
	Carbondale, CO 81623
TELEPHONE:	(970) 963-2209; (800) 437-8675
E-MAIL:	mtsoprisinn@juno.com
WEBSITE:	www.mtsoprisinn.com
ROOMS:	13 Rooms; All with private baths
CHILDREN:	Not allowed
ANIMALS:	Not allowed
HANDICAPPED:	Is handicapped accessible
DIETARY NEEDS:	Will accommodate guests' special dietary needs

Wink's Chili Dip

Makes 3 Cups

1	(3-ounce) package cream cheese, room temperature
1	(4-ounce) can chopped mild green chiles
4	green onions, chopped (reserve 1 teaspoon for garnish)
1	(15-ounce) can Stagg's 99% fat-free chili con carne (do not use chili with a lot of fat; it liquifies on top during baking)
1	(4½-ounce) can chopped black olives (reserve 1 teaspoon for garnish)
¾	cup shredded Monterey Jack or Jack and cheddar mix cheese (reserve 2 teaspoons for garnish)
1	bag lime 'n chile flavored tortilla chips

Preheat oven to 325°F. Coat an 8-inch round, shallow baking dish (which doubles as the serving dish) with nonstick cooking spray. In a medium bowl, combine all of the ingredients, except the tortilla chips and reserved garnish (after combining the ingredients, small pieces of cream cheese should still be visible in the mixture). Pour mixture into the baking dish.

Bake for 35-40 minutes, or until lightly browned and bubbly. Remove from oven; do not stir. Garnish the center of the dip with a sprinkling of the reserved green onions, olives and cheese. Serve hot with tortilla chips.

Eagle Manor

Built in 1917, the Eagle Manor Bed and Breakfast features high ceilings, exquisite oak floors and two fireplaces. Artwork from many of the region's finest artists is prominently displayed on the interior walls. Guest amenities include an indoor swimming pool and sauna, and an outdoor hot tub with privacy fence.

A delicious hearty breakfast is served each morning in the formal dining room. Small group retreats and family reunions are welcome.

INNKEEPERS:	Mike Smith
ADDRESS:	441 Chiquita Lane
	Estes Park, CO 80517
TELEPHONE:	(970) 586-8482; (888) 603-3578
E-MAIL:	mike@eaglemanor.com
WEBSITE:	www.eaglemanor.com
ROOMS:	4 Rooms; All with private baths
CHILDREN:	Welcome
ANIMALS:	Not allowed
HANDICAPPED:	Limited accessibility
DIETARY NEEDS:	Will accommodate guests' special dietary needs

Caramel Apple Dip

Makes 1½ Cups

To ensure a smooth, creamy caramel mixture, always use good quality, name brand, "original" cream cheese. It is equally important to use fresh, soft brown sugar.

1   **(8-ounce) package cream cheese (not low-fat), room temperature**
1   **cup packed brown sugar**
1   **teaspoon vanilla extract**
Apple slices

In a medium microwaveable bowl, stir together the cream cheese, brown sugar and vanilla. Microwave the mixture for 30 seconds. Stir to mix, then microwave for 30 seconds more. Stir until thoroughly mixed and smooth. Serve the dip at room temperature or chilled, with crisp, freshly-cut apple slices. Refrigerate any leftover dip.

Carol's Corner

This caramel dip is addictive, and the good news – it takes only 2 minutes to prepare! I tested this recipe using different brands of cream cheese and even tried a low-fat variety. Results: The texture of the dip is just not the same when using substitute ingredients, so be sure to follow the above advice.

Purple Mountain Lodge

Purple Mountain Lodge is nestled in the valley that is home to Crested Butte, Colorado. A light, cheerful atmosphere welcomes guests. Rooms are tastefully decorated with antiques and down comforter duvet covers adorned with cheerful plaids, denims and bright floral patterns.

Marilyn Caldwell purchased the Purple Mountain Lodge in 1995. Since then, she's been busily refurbishing the lodge.

INNKEEPERS:	Marilyn Caldwell
ADDRESS:	714 Gothic Avenue; PO Box 547
	Crested Butte, CO 81224
TELEPHONE:	(970) 349-5888; (800) 759-9066
E-MAIL:	mailbox@purple-mountain.com
WEBSITE:	www.purple-mountain.com
ROOMS:	7 Rooms; All with private baths
CHILDREN:	Call ahead
ANIMALS:	Not allowed
HANDICAPPED:	Not handicapped accessible
DIETARY NEEDS:	Will accommodate guests' special dietary needs

Spinach-Wrapped Chicken with Curry Mayonnaise

Makes 3 Dozen Appetizers

These chicken appetizers and mayonnaise dip can be prepared a day in advance.

4   boneless, skinless chicken breasts
1   (15-ounce) can chicken broth
¼   cup soy sauce
1   tablespoon Worcestershire sauce
1   bag ready-to-eat fresh spinach
8   cups boiling water
Curry mayonnaise (recipe below)

In a large skillet, combine chicken breasts, chicken broth, soy sauce and Worcestershire sauce. Bring to a boil over medium heat; cover and lower heat. Simmer until chicken is fork-tender, about 15 minutes. Lift chicken from broth and let cool slightly. Cut chicken into 1-inch chunks.

Place whole spinach leaves in a colander. Pour boiling water over leaves; drain thoroughly, then set aside to cool.

To assemble: Place a chicken chunk at stem end of a spinach leaf. Roll over once, fold leaf in on both sides and continue rolling around chicken. Secure end of leaf with a wooden pick. Refrigerate. Serve with curry mayonnaise for dipping.

Curry mayonnaise:
¼   cup sour cream
2   teaspoons curry powder
2   tablespoons chopped Major Grey's chutney
1   teaspoon orange zest

Mix all ingredients until smooth. Cover and refrigerate for at least 1 hour. Makes about ⅔ cup.

Cattail Creek Inn

Named after eight Colorado creeks, each guestroom at the Cattail Creek Inn is distinctive in its design and view. The large and airy Cabin Creek Room features a pine sleigh bed. Bear, moose and pine cones grace the décor of the Buckhorn Creek Room. Guests can watch the sunset across the Rockies from their private deck in the Grizzly Creek Room.

The Coal Creek Room features a French post king-size bed, vaulted ceiling and marvelous views of the mountains and Cattail Pond.

INNKEEPERS:	Sue & Harold Buchman
ADDRESS:	2665 Abarr Drive
	Loveland, CO 80538
TELEPHONE:	(970) 667-7600; (800) 572-2466
E-MAIL:	info@cattailcreekinn.com
WEBSITE:	www.cattailcreekinn.com
ROOMS:	8 Rooms; All with private baths
CHILDREN:	Children age 14 and older are welcome
ANIMALS:	Not allowed
HANDICAPPED:	Is handicapped accessible
DIETARY NEEDS:	Will accommodate guests' special dietary needs

Sausage Won Tons

Makes 24 Won Tons

A party platter of these special appetizers makes a beautiful presentation.

¾ pound Italian sausage, casings removed
½ cup salsa
2 tablespoons chopped mild green chiles
½ cup (2 ounces) shredded Monterey Jack cheese
1 cup (4 ounces) shredded sharp cheddar cheese
Olive oil for greasing muffin cups
24 won ton skins
Sour cream (about ⅓ cup) for garnish
2 green onions, finely chopped, for garnish

In a large skillet, brown the sausage over medium-high heat, breaking the meat up into small pieces. Remove the sausage with a slotted spoon and place on paper towels, pressing to remove as much grease as possible. Discard grease from the skillet. Return the browned sausage to the skillet. Add salsa, green chiles, Monterey Jack and cheddar cheese. Simmer until mixture thickens, about 5 minutes. Remove from heat and cool to room temperature.

Preheat oven to 350°F. Brush mini-muffin cups with olive oil. Press 1 won ton wrapper into each muffin cup (the edges will have a ruffled effect). Fill each wrapper with 1 generous tablespoon of the cooled sausage mixture. Bake until edges begin to brown, about 5-6 minutes. Transfer the filled wrappers from the muffin cups to a baking sheet. Continue to bake until bottoms are crisp, about 10 minutes more. Place the sausage won ton appetizers on a serving platter. Garnish each with a small dollop of sour cream and a sprinkling of chopped green onion. Serve hot.

Wyman Hotel & Inn

A wedding celebration at the Wyman Hotel & Inn is a wonderful experience. The courtyard, complete with garden arbor, makes the perfect location. The Candlelight Caboose, a converted Southern Pacific caboose furnished with an antique bed from Spain and a romantic, soothing two-person whirlpool tub, allows newlyweds a romantic, private wedding night.

Special elopement and wedding packages are available.

INNKEEPERS:	Lorraine & Tom Lewis
ADDRESS:	1371 Greene Street
	Silverton, CO 81433
TELEPHONE:	(970) 387-5372; (800) 609-7845
E-MAIL:	thewyman@frontier.net
WEBSITE:	www.thewyman.com
ROOMS:	18 Rooms; All with private baths
CHILDREN:	Well-behaved children are welcome
ANIMALS:	Welcome in certain rooms
HANDICAPPED:	Is handicapped accessible
DIETARY NEEDS:	Will accommodate guests' special dietary needs

Bruschetta

Makes About 15 Slices

This delicious, elegant appetizer will really impress your friends and family.

1   (6-ounce) can whole, pitted, ripe black olives, drained
3   cloves garlic (more or less to taste)
2   tablespoons extra virgin olive oil
1   tablespoon fresh lemon juice
1   tablespoon dry white wine
Salt to taste
Black pepper, freshly ground, to taste
2   Roma (or plum) tomatoes, sliced ¼-inch thick
½   cup shredded mozzarella cheese
1   baguette (long, narrow, crusty loaf French bread), sliced on
    the diagonal (about ¾-inch thick)

Preheat broiler. In a blender, combine the olives, garlic, olive oil, lemon juice, white wine, salt and pepper. Blend on medium speed to achieve a rough consistency. Add more olive oil if needed.

Spread olive mixture on baguette slices. Place tomato slices on top of olive mixture; sprinkle with grated cheese.

Place slices under broiler for 3-5 minutes, or until cheese is golden brown.

Porter House

Guests of this beautifully restored 1898 Victorian Inn are transported back to a time when gracious living was predominant. Located in the "Tri-City Region" of Fort Collins, Greeley and Loveland, guests of the Porter House enjoy such pleasures as a walk to Lake Windsor, known for its diverse bird population.

All rooms have queen-size beds, cable TV, luxurious terry robes, down filled comforters, central air conditioning and fresh cut flowers.

INNKEEPERS:	Tom & Marni Schmittling
ADDRESS:	530 Main Street
	Windsor, CO 80550
TELEPHONE:	(970) 686-5793
E-MAIL:	phbbinn@aol.com
WEBSITE:	www.bbonline.com/co/porterhouse
ROOMS:	4 Rooms; 1 Suite; All with private baths
CHILDREN:	Children age 14 and older are welcome
ANIMALS:	Not allowed
HANDICAPPED:	Not handicapped accessible
DIETARY NEEDS:	Will accommodate guests' special dietary needs

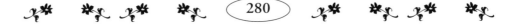

Mediterranean Appetizer

Makes Any Number of Servings

"The hit of a party or gathering! We serve them to our guests with wine in the evening." — Marni Schmittling, Porter House B&B Inn

Sun-dried tomatoes (dried, not oil-packed)
Crusty French bread, sliced into ½-inch slices
Pesto sauce
Feta cheese, crumbled
Greek kalamata olives, pitted and thinly sliced
Parmesan cheese, freshly grated

Preheat oven to 425°F. Bring 2 cups of water to a boil. Submerge sun-dried tomatoes in boiling water for 2 minutes to reconstitute. Drain the tomatoes, cut into slivers and set aside.

Spread about 1 tablespoon of pesto on each slice of bread. Sprinkle 1 tablespoon of crumbled feta cheese on top of the pesto sauce. Add 2-3 slices of Greek olives and some sliced sun-dried tomatoes. Sprinkle with Parmesan cheese. Bake for about 10 minutes, until cheese is melted, checking often to prevent burning. Serve hot.

Ice Palace Inn

Built in 1899, the Ice Palace Inn Bed and Breakfast is located in historic Leadville. Area activities include historical tours, whitewater rafting, gold panning, antique shopping, carriage rides or a trip on the highest standard gauge railroad in the United States.

"Of all the bed and breakfasts we stayed in on our vacation, yours was our favorite. It was charming, divine and luxurious, with the best hospitality."
— Guest, Ice Palace Inn

INNKEEPERS:	Giles & Kami Kolakowski
ADDRESS:	813 Spruce Street
	Leadville, CO 80461
TELEPHONE:	(719) 486-8272; (800) 754-2840
E-MAIL:	icepalace@bwn.net
WEBSITE:	www.icepalaceinn.com
ROOMS:	5 Rooms; All with private baths
CHILDREN:	Welcome
ANIMALS:	Not allowed
HANDICAPPED:	Not handicapped accessible
DIETARY NEEDS:	Will accommodate guests' special dietary needs

Iced Palace Smoothie

Makes 4 Servings

A refreshing and healthful way to start the day!

1   banana
2   **(8-ounce) containers berry yogurt**
1   **cup apricot nectar**
Whipped cream for garnish

Place banana, yogurt and nectar into a blender and process until mixture is smooth. Serve in iced champagne glasses, topped off with whipped cream.

✽ Carol's Corner
This is so easy and so good! Be creative and make your own smoothies by varying the flavor of the yogurt and nectar.

Romantic River Song

Romantic River Song is a small mountain country inn nestled at the foot of Giant Track Mountain in Estes Park. Once a luxurious summer home of the wealthy, that hosted Great Gatsby-like parties, the River Song is now a very special and inviting bed and breakfast inn.

Located at the end of a country lane on 27 wooded acres, guests enjoy the breathtaking panorama of snow-capped peaks in adjacent Rocky Mountain National Park.

INNKEEPERS:	Gary & Sue Mansfield
ADDRESS:	PO Box 1910
	Estes Park, CO 80517
TELEPHONE:	(970) 586-4666
E-MAIL:	romanticriversong@earthlink.net
WEBSITE:	www.romanticriversong.com
ROOMS:	9 Rooms; All with private baths
CHILDREN:	Not allowed
ANIMALS:	Not allowed
HANDICAPPED:	Is handicapped accessible
DIETARY NEEDS:	Call ahead

Banana Mango Smoothie

Makes 6 to 8 Servings

Tall glasses of Banana Mango Smoothies are featured on the cover of this book. This is a healthy, cool and delightful drink for breakfast, or for anytime throughout the day.

3   ripe mangoes
Sugar to taste
4   ripe bananas
1   (2-pound) container low-fat vanilla yogurt
6-8   fresh strawberries

Peel and slice the mangoes. Place in a saucepan with water to cover and bring to boil. Cook until tender, about 20 minutes. Add small amounts of sugar, a little at a time, to sweeten, if they're too tart.

Put mangoes into blender, reserving the juice. Add bananas and yogurt. Blend until smooth, adding a little mango juice, if the mixture is too thick. Chill. Stir and pour into serving glasses. Garnish with a strawberry on the rim of each glass.

Last Dollar Inn

B uilt in 1898, the Last Dollar Inn Bed and Breakfast is located in Cripple Creek. Historic mines shaft and cabins still dot the local landscape. Modern-day miners scoop ore-laden earth in trucks and haul it to the local gold processing plant, a far cry from the pioneer days when Bob Womack started a gold rush that caught the world's attention.

Despite his discovery, Bob Womack died impoverished. But the gold rush he started left a legacy that lives on today.

INNKEEPERS:	Rick & Janice Wood
ADDRESS:	315 East Carr Avenue
	Cripple Creek, CO 80813
TELEPHONE:	(719) 689-9113; (888) 429-6700
E-MAIL:	packy578@concentric.net
WEBSITE:	www.cripple-creek.co.us/lastdinn.htm
ROOMS:	6 Rooms; All with private baths
CHILDREN:	Not allowed
ANIMALS:	Not allowed
HANDICAPPED:	Not handicapped accessible
DIETARY NEEDS:	Will accommodate guests' special dietary needs

Last Dollar Mocha Coffee

Makes 2¾ Cups Mix, Enough for About 20 Cups of Coffee

Try this warm, soothing beverage whenever you feel like pampering someone special, including yourself!

½	cup instant coffee granules
1	cup hot chocolate mix powder
2	tablespoons unsweetened cocoa powder
1	cup non-dairy creamer
⅔	cup sugar

Combine all of the ingredients in a blender (or coffee grinder) and process to a fine powder. Store the mocha coffee mix in a labeled, airtight jar.

To serve: Add 2 to 3 heaping teaspoons of mix to 1 cup of hot water. Stir thoroughly, sip and enjoy!

Cheyenne Canon Inn

THE CHEYENNE CAÑON INN

Located at the entrance to Cheyenne Canon Park, the Cheyenne Canon Inn offers beautiful views and convenient access to some of the area's most spectacular hiking, biking and driving tours. Built in 1918, the inn was an upscale bordello, gambling casino and music hall until 1930.

Every morning, a full gourmet breakfast is served either on the massive oak table in the dining room or on the front veranda. An afternoon reception features fine wines and appetizers.

INNKEEPERS:	Keith Hampton & Alicia Bixby
ADDRESS:	2030 West Cheyenne Boulevard
	Colorado Springs, CO 80906
TELEPHONE:	(719) 633-0625
E-MAIL:	info@cheyennecanoninn.com
WEBSITE:	www.cheyennecanoninn.com
ROOMS:	9 Rooms; 1 Suite; 1 Cottage; All with private baths
CHILDREN:	Welcome
ANIMALS:	Not allowed
HANDICAPPED:	Not handicapped accessible
DIETARY NEEDS:	Will accommodate guests' special dietary needs

Ginger Cream Scones

Makes 8 Scones

Delightfully different, these scones are special! When making this recipe, allow 20 extra minutes, as the dough needs time to rest before baking.

1½   cups all-purpose flour
¼   cup sugar
1½   teaspoons baking powder
⅛   teaspoon salt
1   cup heavy whipping cream
2-3 tablespoons finely minced, peeled fresh ginger
2   tablespoons butter
2   tablespoons brown sugar

In a large bowl, sift together the flour, sugar, baking powder and salt. In a medium bowl, beat cream until soft peaks form. Fold the whipped cream into the dry ingredients.

On a lightly floured surface, knead the dough gently until it starts to hold together. Add the minced ginger. Knead a few more times until the ginger is evenly distributed and the dough is nearly smooth. Divide dough in half. Form two 5-inch rounds (each about ¾-inch thick). Cut each round into quarters. Place the wedges on an ungreased cookie sheet. Let dough rest for 20 minutes.

Preheat oven to 425°F. In a small saucepan (or in a small dish in the microwave), melt the butter with the brown sugar; whisk until thoroughly combined. Brush the butter mixture onto the tops of the scones. Bake for 15-20 minutes, or until light golden. Serve hot from the oven or at room temperature.

San Sophia Inn

B uilt in 1988, on the former site of the 1890's Telluride Stables, the
San Sophia is one of the finest inns in the western United States.
Designed exclusively as an inn for the discriminating traveler, all rooms are
named after former gold and silver mines in the area. The dining area
offers spectacular views of Ajax Peak and Telluride Mountain.

Amenities include a full gourmet breakfast and an afternoon reception that
features appetizers, fine wines and micro-brewery beers.

INNKEEPERS:	Keith Hampton & Alicia Bixby
ADDRESS:	330 West Pacific
	Telluride, CO 81435
TELEPHONE:	(970) 728-3001
E-MAIL:	info@sansophia.com
WEBSITE:	www.sansophia.com
ROOMS:	16 Rooms; 15 Condominiums; Private baths
CHILDREN:	Welcome
ANIMALS:	Not allowed
HANDICAPPED:	Not handicapped accessible
DIETARY NEEDS:	Will accommodate guests' special dietary needs

Citrus Tomato Bisque

Makes 4 Main Course or 6 First Course Servings

During the holidays, garnish this soup with fresh cilantro for a festive look.

1	tablespoon butter
1	large onion, coarsely chopped
3	cloves garlic, minced
2	pounds tomatoes, peeled, seeds removed and coarsely chopped*
4	cups (1 quart) chicken broth
1½	cups heavy cream

Grated zest of 2 oranges
Salt and pepper to taste
Juice from 2 oranges

In a very large skillet or stockpot, melt the butter. Add the onion, garlic and tomatoes; sauté until onions are translucent.

Add the stock, cream and orange zest. Simmer for 20-30 minutes, then cool slightly. Carefully transfer the hot soup to a blender. Purée until smooth. Season with salt and pepper. Add orange juice; stir well. Heat through and serve hot.

*Note: To peel the tomatoes, cut a shallow X in the bottom of each tomato. Place the tomatoes into boiling water for about 15 seconds. Remove the tomatoes; transfer to a bowl of ice water. The skins will pull off or will remove easily with a knife.

> *Carol's Corner*
> *The San Sophia serves this distinctive soup hot, but I also tasted it chilled – it's wonderful either way. I suggest making the soup a day in advance for full flavor development, as the citrus taste becomes more pronounced. Another advantage to preparing the soup ahead, there will be no messy kitchen when dinner guests arrive. To serve the soup hot, just gently reheat it on the stove.*

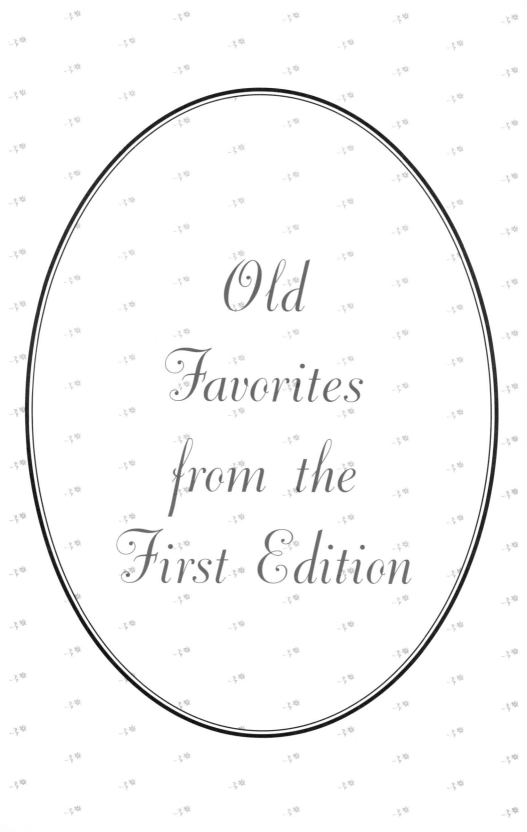

Old

Favorites

from the

First Edition

Chocolate Covered Strawberries

Makes 12 Strawberries

The Sterling House says, "For a light dessert, this recipe is easy and very romantic. It is also great for afternoon teas."

½   cup chocolate chips
1   tablespoon oil
12   strawberries
Chocolate sprinkles (optional)
White chocolate chips (optional)

Over a double broiler or in a microwave, melt chocolate chips until smooth, stirring every 30 seconds until melted. Add oil and mix well.

Wash and dry strawberries. Hold them by their stems and dip them into the chocolate mixture. Shake off excess. Roll in chocolate sprinkles, if desired. Lay on wax paper and refrigerate for 1 hour, or until chocolate is firm. You can vary this recipe by using the white chocolate as well.

Carol's Corner

We had lots of fun experimenting with this recipe. We used several different fruits and "double dipped" in both kinds of chocolate. Some favorites: Strawberries – dip in chocolate, then dip again (just the tip) in white chocolate; Golden delicious apples – dip halfway in chocolate, then drizzle with white chocolate; Oranges slices – dip halfway in white chocolate, drizzle with chocolate; Almonds – dip the pointed ends in the chocolate. Great!

Four Fruit Compote

Makes 12 to 16 Servings

1	(20-ounce) can pineapple chunks or tidbits
½	cup sugar
2	tablespoons cornstarch
⅓	cup orange juice
1	tablespoon lemon juice
1	(11-ounce) can mandarin oranges, drained
3-4	unpeeled apples, chopped (use a mix of red and green for color)
2-3	bananas, sliced

Drain pineapple, reserving ¾ cup juice. In a saucepan, combine sugar and cornstarch. Add pineapple juice, orange juice and lemon juice. Cook and stir over medium heat until thickened and bubbly; cook and stir for 1 more minute. Remove from heat; set aside.

In a bowl, combine pineapple chunks, oranges, apples and bananas. Pour warm sauce over the fruit; stir gently to coat. Cover and refrigerate.

Make-ahead tip: The compote, except for the bananas, can be made a day in advance. Add the bananas just before serving.

> *Carol's Corner*
> *Refreshing! This citrus glaze is a wonderful complement to the medley of fruit. It would also be great to use fresh fruits in season. Braeburn apples are especially wonderful for the recipe … crunchy!*

Blueberry Cream Muffins

Makes 12 Muffins

2	eggs
1	cup sugar
½	cup oil
½	teaspoon vanilla extract
2	cups flour
½	teaspoon salt
½	teaspoon baking soda
1	teaspoon baking powder
1	cup sour cream
1	cup fresh blueberries

Preheat oven to 400°F. Grease and flour 12 muffin cups. In a large bowl, beat eggs and slowly add sugar. While beating, slowly add oil and vanilla.

Sift together flour, salt, baking soda and baking powder. Add dry ingredients alternately with sour cream to the egg mixture. Gently fold in the blueberries. Spoon batter into prepared muffin cups. Bake for about 20 minutes.

Note: These muffins are outstanding with fresh berries. If you use frozen blueberries, do not let them thaw, and add 5-8 minutes to the baking time.

Southern Biscuit Muffins

Makes 12 Muffins

Easy to make at the last minute!

2½	cups flour
¼	cup sugar
1½	tablespoons baking powder
¾	cup (1½ sticks) cold butter
1	cup cold milk

Preheat oven to 400°F. Grease and flour 12 muffin cups. These muffins brown better on the sides and bottom when baked without paper liners.

In a large bowl, combine the flour, sugar and baking powder. Using a pastry blender, cut in butter until mixture resembles coarse crumbs. Stir in milk just until mixture is moistened. Spoon into muffin cups. Bake for 18-20 minutes, or until golden. Remove from pan. Serve hot.

Carol's Corner
With a light sweet taste, these biscuits are delicious! Soft and fluffy on the inside, light brown and crunchy on the outside.

Pumpkin Granola Pancakes

Makes 12-16 Pancakes

2   cups baking mix (such as Bisquick)
2   tablespoons packed brown sugar
2   teaspoons cinnamon
1   teaspoon allspice
1   (12-ounce) can evaporated milk
½   cup canned pumpkin
2   tablespoons vegetable oil
2   eggs
1   teaspoon vanilla extract
Granola (one with raisins is especially good)
Maple syrup for serving
Applesauce for serving

Preheat an oiled griddle or skillet. Combine baking mix, brown sugar, cinnamon and allspice. Add evaporated milk, pumpkin, oil, eggs and vanilla. Beat until smooth.

Preheat oven to 200°F. Using a ¼ cup measure, pour batter onto hot griddle or skillet. Sprinkle some granola on top of batter. Cook until bubbly on top. Turn and cook until done. Remove pancakes from griddle and keep warm in the oven while making remaining pancakes. Serve with maple syrup and hot applesauce.

French Toast New Orleans

Makes 2 Servings

2   eggs
½   cup milk
4   slices French bread
Pralines (recipe below)
Maple syrup for serving

Preheat the broiler. Preheat an oiled, oven-proof skillet. In a medium bowl, beat together eggs and milk. Soak the bread in the mixture. Cook bread in hot skillet until golden brown. Turn slices over. When cooked on both sides, spread on praline mixture and place frying pan with French toast under the broiler until mixture is bubbling. (If your pan is not ovenproof, transfer the French toast to a baking sheet and place under the broiler.) Serve with maple syrup.

Pralines:

¼   cup packed brown sugar
2   tablespoons chopped pecans
1   tablespoon butter
1   teaspoon vanilla extract

Combine all ingredients in a microwaveable bowl and warm in microwave or heat in a saucepan on stove. Stir until ingredients are mixed and smooth.

WPR Frittata

Makes 6 to 8 Servings

For a small gathering, this recipe can easily be cut in half and baked in an 11x7-inch baking dish for 30-35 minutes. Note: This dish needs to be refrigerated overnight.

1-2	(7-ounce) cans diced green chiles
6	flour tortillas
4	cups (16 ounces) shredded Monterey Jack cheese
10	large eggs
¾	cup half & half
½	teaspoon ground cumin
½	teaspoon onion salt
½	teaspoon garlic salt
½	teaspoon black pepper
½	teaspoon salt

Salsa for serving

Preheat oven to 350°F. Lightly oil a 13x9-inch baking dish. Spread one can of green chiles on the bottom of the pan (or ½ can if using just one can of chiles). Top with 3 tortillas, tearing or cutting them into 1x1-inch pieces. Add 2 cups of the cheese. Repeat layers (chiles, tortillas, cheese).

Whisk eggs and half & half together. Add cumin, onion salt, garlic salt, pepper and salt to the egg mixture and mix well. Slowly pour egg mixture over the ingredients in the baking dish. Cover and refrigerate overnight. Uncover and bake for 45 minutes, or until lightly browned and bubbly. Cool for 5-10 minutes and cut into serving pieces. Serve with salsa.

Mexican Eggs

Makes 4 Servings

Note: This recipe can be doubled and baked in a 13x9-inch baking dish. It will then serve 8-10.

8	ounces (1 cup) small curd cottage cheese
5	eggs, lightly beaten
1	(4-ounce) can green chiles, drained
2	cups (8-ounces) shredded Monterey Jack cheese, shredded
2	tablespoons flour
2	tablespoons butter, melted
½	teaspoon baking powder

Sour cream for serving
Salsa for serving

Preheat oven to 400°F. Coat a 9-inch pie pan with nonstick cooking spray. In a large bowl, mix together all ingredients. Pour into the pie pan. Bake for 10 minutes.

Lower oven temperature to 350°F and continue baking for 20 minutes more, or until center is set. Serve with sour cream and salsa.

Huevos Rancheros

Makes 4 Servings

Serve with fresh, homemade sopapillas!

1   pound bulk breakfast sausage
1   (10-ounce) can enchilada sauce
4   eggs, fried or poached
4   flour tortillas, warmed
Onion, chopped
Shredded cheddar cheese
Lettuce, chopped
Guacamole
Homemade sopapillas (optional; recipe below)

Cook, drain and crumble the sausage. Add the enchilada sauce to the cooked sausage and warm until heated through. Fry or poach the eggs.

Layer in this order on warm plates:
Tortilla
Sausage and enchilada sauce mixture
Onion
Cheese
Fried or poached egg
More cheese
Lettuce
Guacamole

Optional: place in preheated 300°F oven until cheese is melted.

Homemade sopapillas:

Thaw frozen bread dough and break off small pieces. Roll very thinly and drop into hot oil in a deep fat fryer or a deep skillet. Turn as soon as bottom side is golden and fry the other side (they will puff up). Drain on paper towels. Serve with honey, jam, or butter.

Corn Casserole

Makes 12 Servings

This is just a great buffet or potluck dish to take to your next party — everyone raves about it.

2	cans (14-ounce) creamed corn
2	cans (15-ounce) whole kernel corn, drained
1	medium onion, chopped and sautéed
½	cup butter, melted
4	teaspoons sugar

White pepper to taste

2	eggs, beaten
48	saltine crackers, crushed
2	cups (8 ounces) shredded cheddar cheese
1	jar (4-ounce) pimentos, chopped
1⅓	cups milk

Preheat oven to 350°F. Coat a 13x9-inch baking dish with nonstick cooking spray. In a large bowl, mix all ingredients together. Bake for 45 minutes, or until light brown and bubbly.

Make-ahead tip: This dish can be made in advance and refrigerated or frozen until ready to bake. May need to bake for 5-10 minutes longer.

Carol's Corner
I made this one day when I was in a hurry and didn't take the time to sauté the onion – it's great that way, too! An easy way to crush the crackers is in your hands as you're adding them to the bowl.

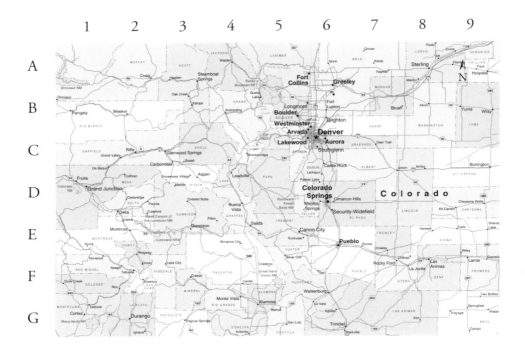

B&B Locations

Alphabetical Listing of B&Bs

Index

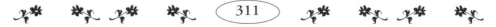

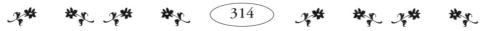

About the Authors

Carol McCollum Faino, an Iowa native and former teacher, started cooking as a young girl. Her creative cooking efforts were first publicly recognized when she received the Home Economics Superintendent's Award as a high school senior. She devoted much time to perfecting these winning skills by attending cooking classes, while raising three children, teaching and moving 14 times in 30 years with her husband, a Navy pilot. Carol and her husband, Rod, enjoy traveling, seeking out new bed & breakfasts and collecting simple, yet sensational recipes. They reside in Castle Rock, Colorado.

Doreen Kaitfors Hazledine is a former Mrs. South Dakota who traveled extensively, gave inspirational speeches and was named an Outstanding Young Woman of America. Before starting a writing career, she was a teacher and businesswoman and was listed as an honored professional in the National Register's WHO's WHO in Executives and Professionals. Her varied writing talents range from travel writing to inspirational nonfiction to screenwriting. A Hollywood producer optioned one of her screenplays.

Carol and Doreen are the authors of the *Colorado Bed & Breakfast Cookbook*, the *Washington State Bed & Breakfast Cookbook* and the *California Wine Country Bed & Breakfast Cookbook and Travel Guide*.

3D Press Book Catalog

Boulder Cooks
Recipes and Profiles from Boulder County's Best Kitchens
$18.95 / 204pp / 0-9634607-8-1

Denver Hiking Guide
45 Hikes within 45 Minutes of Denver.
$12.95 / 104pp / ISBN 1-889593-58-3

Colorado Bed & Breakfast Cookbook
From the Warmth & Hospitality of 88 Colorado B&B's and
Country Inns
$19.95 / 320pp / ISBN 0-9653751-0-2

Colorado Farmers' Market Cookbook
200 Recipes Fresh From Colorado's Farmers' Markets & Chefs
$18.95 / 224pp / ISBN 1-889593-00-1

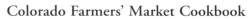

Colorado Month-to-Month Gardening
A Practical Guide for Designing, Growing and Maintaining
Your Colorado Garden
$19.95 / 162pp / ISBN 1-889593-01-X

Month-to-Month Gardening Utah
Tips for Designing, Growing and Maintaining Your Utah Garden
$16.95 / 156pp / ISBN 1-889593-03-6

Month-to-Month Gardening New Mexico
Tips for Designing, Growing and Maintaining Your New
Mexico Garden
$16.95 / 156pp / ISBN 1-889593-02-8

Washington State Bed & Breakfast
From the Warmth & Hospitality of 85 B&B's and Country
Inns throughout Washington State.
$21.95 / 320pp / ISBN 0-9653751-9-6

3D Press Order Form

4340 E. KENTUCKY AVE., Suite 446
DENVER, CO 80246
888-456-3607

PLEASE SEND ME:	Price	Quantity
BOULDER COOKS	$18.95	_____
COLORADO BED & BREAKFAST COOKBOOK	$19.95	_____
COLORADO FARMERS' MARKET COOKBOOK	$18.95	_____
COLORADO MONTH-TO-MONTH GARDENING	$19.95	_____
DENVER HIKING GUIDE	$12.95	_____
MONTH-TO-MONTH GARDENING UTAH	$16.95	_____
WASHINGTON BED & BREAKFAST COOKBOOK	$21.95	_____

SUBTOTAL: $_____

Colorado residents add 3.8% sales tax. $_____

Add $4.50 for shipping for 1st book, add $1 for each additional $_____

TOTAL ENCLOSED: $_____

SEND TO:

Name_____

Address _____

City _____State _____Zip _____

Gift From _____

We accept checks, money orders, Visa or Mastercard (please include expiration date). Please make checks payable to 3D Press, Inc. Sorry, no COD orders.

Please charge my ☐ VISA ☐ MASTERCARD

Card Number _____ Expiration Date_____

Cardholder's Signature _____

CALL TOLL FREE 888-456-3607 FOR MORE INFORMATION

3D Press Book Catalog

Boulder Cooks
Recipes and Profiles from Boulder County's Best Kitchens
$18.95 / 204pp / 0-9634607-8-1

Denver Hiking Guide
45 Hikes within 45 Minutes of Denver.
$12.95 / 104pp / ISBN 1-889593-58-3

Colorado Bed & Breakfast Cookbook
From the Warmth & Hospitality of 88 Colorado B&B's and
Country Inns
$19.95 / 320pp / 0-9653751-0-2

Colorado Farmers' Market Cookbook
200 Recipes Fresh From Colorado's Farmers' Markets & Chefs
$18.95 / 224 pp / ISBN 1-889593-00-1

Colorado Month-to-Month Gardening
A Practical Guide for Designing, Growing and Maintaining
Your Colorado Garden
$19.95 / 162pp / ISBN 1-889593-01-X

Month-to-Month Gardening Utah
Tips for Designing, Growing and Maintaining Your Utah Garden
$16.95 / 162pp / ISBN 1-889593-03-6

Month-to-Month Gardening New Mexico
Tips for Designing, Growing and Maintaining Your New
Mexico Garden
$16.95 / ISBN 1-889593-02-8 / $16.95

Washington State Bed & Breakfast
From the Warmth & Hospitality of 85 B&B's and Country
Inns throughout Washington State.
$21.95 / ISBN 0-9653751-9-6 / 320pp

3D Press Order Form

4340 E. KENTUCKY AVE., Suite 446
DENVER, CO 80246
888-456-3607

PLEASE SEND ME:	Price	Quantity
BOULDER COOKS	$18.95	_____
COLORADO BED & BREAKFAST COOKBOOK	$19.95	_____
COLORADO FARMERS' MARKET COOKBOOK	$18.95	_____
COLORADO MONTH-TO-MONTH GARDENING	$19.95	_____
DENVER HIKING GUIDE	$12.95	_____
MONTH-TO-MONTH GARDENING UTAH	$16.95	_____
WASHINGTON BED & BREAKFAST COOKBOOK	$21.95	_____

SUBTOTAL: $_____

Colorado residents add 3.8% sales tax. $_____

Add $4.50 for shipping for 1st book, add $1 for each additional $_____

TOTAL ENCLOSED: $_____

SEND TO:

Name_____

Address _____

City _____State _____Zip_____

Gift From _____

We accept checks, money orders, Visa or Mastercard (please include expiration date). Please make checks payable to 3D Press, Inc. Sorry, no COD orders.

Please charge my ☐ VISA ☐ MASTERCARD

Card Number _____ Expiration Date_____

Cardholder's Signature _____

CALL TOLL FREE 888-456-3607 FOR MORE INFORMATION